MY LIFE WAS A

Sideshow

THE BIOGRAPHY OF

WENDELL SAWYER

ORIGINAL MEMBER OF
LEGENDARY VOCAL GROUP

BLUE MAGIC

AS TOLD TO

ANTHONY "TONY" JOHNSON

This publication contains the opinions and ideas of its author. It is intended to provide helpful and informative material on the subjects addressed in the publication. The author and publisher specifically disclaim all responsibility for any liability, loss or risk, personal or otherwise, which is incurred as a consequence, directly or indirectly, of the use and application of any of the contents of this book.

WORKBOOK PRESS LLC
187 E Warm Springs Rd,
Suite B285 Las Vegas NV 89119 USA
Website: https://workbookpress.com/
Hotline: 1-888-818-4856
Email: admin@workbookpress.com

Ordering Information:
Quantity sales. Special discounts are available on quantity purchases by corporations, associations, and others. For details, contact the publisher at the address above.

ISBN-13:   978-1-965732-72-4 Paperback Version
                978-1-965732-73-1 Digital Version

PUB. DATE: 04/24/2025

" SIDESHOW "

My Life Was A Sideshow.
The Biography Of Wendell Sawyer
A Member Of The Famous Singing Group
"Blue Magic"

As told to   xxx

ANTHONY "TONY" JOHNSON

TABLE OF CONTENTS

THE WRITER'S COMMENTS AND ACKNOWLEDGEMENTS

I alike so many others grew up listening to the music of Blue Magic. You can only imagine my surprise when Wendell asked me to help him tell his story after meeting him through a mutual friend, and after he became familiar with my previously published book. Sometimes while working on this Project, we became just two old Philly boys talking.

It takes courage to share your fortunes, mistakes, and inner most feelings with the world. Wendell has shown such courage. From rags to riches to rags he tells his story in detail. His struggled like so many people with illicit drug use was monumental. His religious beliefs and spirituality are to be admired. They were a part of the good versus evil in that him, that I personally could relate to in my own life. When you take into consideration that he had no mentors to guide and advise him along the way, especially on financial matters, other than a brief encounter with a man he called Dr. York. I had to admire his ability to have survived for decades in the" dog eat dog" world of the music business. His life in many ways was trial by fire.

While writing this book I realized how different our environments were during our formative years while at the same time there were some similarities. There is only a couple of years difference in our ages. I was born and raised in Philadelphia also just a different area. My high school Germantown High played his high school Ben Franklin in sports so I was quite familiar with the area in which he lived. My maternal grandparents lived not that far from the areas he described in the book. I jokingly asked him during one of our sessions was he one of the boys that chased me out of the neighborhood when I ventured there to visit several different girls? I hoped that in sharing his story it would in some way be a cathartic experience for him as I felt his pain when he talked about some of the difficult times in his life.

The music of Blue Magic was a bridge between the doo wop singing of the 50's. Motown of the 60's. R&B music was a natural progression in the 70's and 80's. Wendell's definition of "Soul Music" and why he thinks it will survive came from his heart. His explanation as to why the era of the balladeer ended with the creation of "Disco music" was educational.

I would like to thank my sister Angela Shaw and a lifelong friend Malcolm McGraw who were willing to take the personal time to read the manuscript and give me constructive suggestions. I would like to thank my wife Denise for putting up with countless hours spent in our home working on this book. Thanks also for the food you cooked for Wendell and myself, while we were working.

Chapter 1
"We're On The Right Track"

"We sometimes do not look at life for what it is but after you have lived a certain number of years you can look back and see how the things you have experienced are interconnected!"

Wendell Sawyer

I was born in 1951 to Mattie Lee Tyson and Weldon James Sawyer in Mount Vernon New York.

Both of my parents were from North Carolina but did not meet until they moved, north and settled in Mount Vernon New York. My father was from Roper North Carolina, and my mother was from Oak City, North Carolina a small town, Northwest of Charlotte. They were both in their early 20's when they met. My father prided himself in looking like money with his silky slicked back hair. He was a womanizer, who got married for the first time at the age of 18. Women were always after him. He also was a good dancer. He said that he used to frequent the Audubon Ballroom in Harlem and that his favorite dance was the Lindy Hop.

My father told me that he was hanging out with a friend by the name of Johnny who invited him to go to a house with him to visit a friend. This is where he first met my mother. At that time, my mother was employed in the home as a maid. They were both instantly attracted to each other and began dating. Eventually, my mother became pregnant with me.

They had been dating for about a year and so they decided to get married. My mother told me that she was told by a doctor that she could not have children because her uterus was stretched, possibly from her being forced to pull a plow as a young girl on a North Carolina farm as a young girl. The doctor who gave her that information obviously did not know what he was talking about because my mother ended up having four children. She told me that the day I was born I had white skin and blue eyes. I know that I have white ancestors in my family, as do many African Americans. That bit of information was hard for me to believe. Things were fine between my parents until my father, who had previously been married got into trouble because he owed back child support. I have three older brothers from my father previous relationship. They are Rinaco, Wellington, and Ronald Sawyer. I did not have any contact with these brothers while growing up but I do remember seeing a picture of one of them in our apartment. My mother did explain to me that they were my older brothers.

In order to escape the law, my dad moved from the home and relocated to Philadelphia, Pennsylvania. By this time my brother Vernon was born. I remember sitting on the steps outside of my basement apartment many times, it seemed like all day, after he left waiting for him to come home. He never did. My mother would always come outside, and bring me back into our apartment. She, in a nurturing way, tried to explain to me the reason my father was not coming home. I did not understand and just believed he did not love me. I just wanted to see him. Years later, during one of our talks, when I was an adult I told him about the disappointment that I felt when he never showed up. He just laughed. That hurt me deeply as he just ignored my feelings on that subject.

Believe it or not I have vivid memories of things that happened even at very early age. I remember sitting in a crib while watching my mother's little dog run around the room. I remember watching different people come in and go out of our basement apartment. My crib was positioned just below the front window. I remember seeing people as they approached our front door.

Eventually my father sent my mother a letter telling her to come to Philadelphia, where he now had an apartment set up for the whole family. My mother packed her bags, and with me walking and Vernon in her arms boarded the train at Penn Station in New York City. We got off the train at 30th Street Station in Philadelphia. I remember stepping off the train while holding my mother's hand and getting caught between the space in the platform and the train. My mother was holding my brother Vernon in one arm and bags in the same hand, while trying to hold onto me with her other hand. She screamed for help that never came. Her maternal instincts took over and she managed to pull me from that space just before the train pulled off. That was an early experience that I will never forget. I also believe that this was my first brush with death.

I do not remember where we lived upon arriving in Philadelphia. I do know that it was in North Philadelphia. My father set up the place for my mother Vernon and myself.

He did not live there with us. I do not remember ever seeing him visit. He did tell my mother that he was promised another apartment that was much larger. He kept that promise five months later.

My family moved next to 856 N 20th Street in North Philadelphia. A lady by the name of Ruth had an apartment on the second floor of her house for rent. Ruth was my father's friend. I remember her because I thought she was a pretty woman. My father still did not live with us but he would come by to visit.

Our neighbor had an adopted daughter. One day my mother put Vernon and I in the back yard to play unsupervised. This girl, who was about 12 years old, came out into the yard and convinced Vernon and I to come to her bedroom. Once we were in her room, she had us take off all our clothes. She first had me then Vernon gets on top of her. I had no idea what was going on but I followed her instructions. I did ask her why she wanted me to do that. She responded by saying that she wanted my milk. I did not know what she meant, but I did what she wanted anyway. My mother went to check on us. When were not in the yard, she went to the girl's room just in time to witness my brother and I being molested. She quickly gathered our clothes together and got us out of the room. That evening she told Miss Ruth what happened. Later that same evening, I heard that girl yelling in pain as she was tied to a pole in the basement and beaten by mother who adopted her. This was my first Introduction to sex.

There was another girl in my neighborhood who would take me over to her house and pull out my penis. Many years later I questioned myself as to why I was chosen by these girls for sexual encounters at such an early age. Did they take advantage of the fact that I was naïve? Was it because I was available? I have never been able to figure out, why me?

I was four or five years old, and all I remember doing was watching television. One of my favorite shows was The Three Stooges. Watching slap stick comedy antics at that young age had me believe that I could perform what I saw without injury to anyone. No one told me that what I watched was not real. On one occasion, Vernon took a toy that I was playing with from me. When he would not give me the toy back, I proceeded to pick up a hammer and hit him in the head, thinking that the result was going to be the same as that of my television heroes. The problem was that this hammer was not made of soft rubber like the ones the stooges used. This was a real metal hammer. To my surprise the result was not the same as what I saw on television. My brother started crying while seriously bleeding. My mom rushed in, picked him up and patched him up. Life moved on in the Sawyer home.

My mother was a very spiritual woman. All that I learned about God and religion at that time was from her.

We next moved to 844 N 20th street in North Philadelphia where I used to watch my mother pacing back and forth in the apartment talking to herself out loud and praying to God. I remember during one Christmas season, I heard her say to God, while sitting at a table crying, that she had no money to buy gifts for her children for Christmas. I went into another room where there was a big mirror on the wall, and while standing in front of the mirror I asked God to let my mother hit the number. She hit the number the next day. I never told her about my speaking to God. Since it worked that time, I tried praying to God again a week later. I followed the same routine as before standing in front of the mirror for a second time. It worked before so I did not see any reason why it would not work again. My mother hit the number again. I backed off after my mother hit the number the second time thinking I had better save my future prayers for an emergency.

Another unexplained spiritual thing that happened was the medical condition my youngest brother Michael suffered from at birth. My mother told me when he was born his heart was outside his rib cage. She called it a" dead basket" because she could see his heart beating through the blanket that covered him. She told me that she put her hands on his heart and prayed. God answered her prayer when according to her Michael's heart went back into the normal position in his chest. The doctors could never explain this phenomenon. I believe the powers we possess with the help of God are sometimes unexplainable. Those two experiences made me believe that there are amazing higher forces in the universe. I believe children are pure in heart. That purity was my connection to the spiritual world as a young child.

My maternal grandfather Clarence Tyson was a bounty hunter in North Carolina. He did this work in and around the Elizabeth City area. For every person who was wanted black or white that he brought back to the local police they gave him five acres of land rather than money. Over the years he accumulated a great deal of money from that land ownership. My maternal aunt Lily was into "roots" healing. Many rural black people were compelled to used alternative medical practices because there were no black doctors and very few white ones. Because of this situation they adapted by learning ways to heal themselves and their families.

When my mother and father were together, every summer they would drive the family down to my grandfather's farm. I remember him living in a big house with a wood burning stove and an outhouse as a bathroom. I was a city kid so all of this was foreign to me. On his farm he grew tobacco, corn, tomatoes, peas and just about any other vegetables that you can imagine. Chickens roamed freely in front of his house. We used to pick the worms off the tobacco before storing it in a warehouse. I remember one time he took me to the local store and pulled out a wad of money so thick that I had never seen anything like it before. He gave me a dollar" here boy, go get yourself something!" I must admit that I thought to myself "you only gave me a dollar out of all that money you have in your pocket."

When I was around seven or eight years old, my maternal grandmother and my aunt Lily were invited up for a visit. Aunt Mamie, who was one my mother's other sister already lived in Philadelphia. Aunt Lily lived on the family farm in her own house. When my grandmother decided to visit again the next summer, there was talk that aunt Lily wanted to take over the farm. There were disagreements between aunt Lily and my grandfather about how the farm should be run. Sometime after that last visit to Philadelphia it was alleged that my grandfather fell out of a tree and sustained fatal injuries. He did not die immediately, so while in a coma there were questions as to why a man of his age would climb up into a tree. It was rumored that aunt Lily had something to do with his death.

My parents were a TRIP! The first time I saw them fight was over a phone call. The phone rang and first my father said that it is for him. Mom replied" No, it is for me." My mother got to the phone first and started talking. I guessed that the phone call was for her because she talked on the phone like she knew who it was. My father got mad and yanked the phone cord out of the wall. Mom then took the phone and hit him in the head. Blood shot out of his head as he ran out into the street yelling "She is trying to kill me she is trying to kill me!"

There was another occasion when I was around nine, that they started physically fighting. My mother fell behind the couch, during the fight and although I could not see everything that was happening, I did see my father was punching her with his fist.

I found out later in life that my mother put my father out because she found out through a neighbor, that she could get more money from welfare if there was no man in the house. Once I found out this information it just reinforced how I already felt about the system in America which was structured to destroy the black family. Boys were hurt the most by this rule. We needed and still need our black fathers, grandfathers, and uncles to be in of our lives.

For the most part my other three siblings and I got

along well. My sister Lorraine who was the third child born in my family and I did have our share of brother, sister arguments. My sister was a tattletale. That caused problems between us. Vernon and I often teased her about her behavior. On one occasion she told dad that I did something that I did not do. He beat me so bad that my mother had to stop him. I then wanted to get my sister for telling a lie that got me spanked. As soon as Lorraine came out of the room she was in, I jumped on her. My father saw me attack her and beat me again.

My youngest brother Michael and I were so far apart in age that we were never close. I wish now that we could have been closer. Vernon and I did not pay much attention to him because of the differences in our ages. Years later it hurt me when I found out that he could not read. I believe that Lorraine, who took care of him most of the time, did his homework and other things to help him get through school. It was hard for me to visualize someone getting to high school and not be able to read. He was proof positive that a school system could push a kid through school, allowing the person to be illiterate.

While we were all living together as a family at 844 N. 20th Street, there was a lady who moved on the third floor by the name of Rose. Rose had a boyfriend. I remember him as being a very big man. One day he got into an argument with my father. I do not remember what the dispute was about. My siblings and I had gone out with our mother. When we returned home as we approached our front door, I watched my mother as she looked up through the shadow behind the blinds on the first floor. She saw what appeared to be a large man holding a hatchet over my father as he sat in a chair. We all ran inside the house where I saw my father trying to hold him off with his hands. Mom interceded pulling the man off my dad. The big man then retreated to his apartment. I never found out what the argument was about, but my father got in to arguments all the time with people.

There was another time when a guy said something to my mother that my father did not like. He and the man were up in each other faces when my father pulled out what police used to call a "slapper" and knocked the guy through a wall. A slapper was a small piece of metal wrapped in leather. Police were famous for carrying them at that time.

Around my age of nine my father wanted to visit New York. He decided that he would take me with him. Upon arriving at our destination in New York, he parked his car on a hill, with the vehicle pointed down the hill towards a busy highway. He then told me to stay in the car, while he went into a house across the street. I am now in the car by myself. Twenty minutes after sitting in the car by myself with nothing to do, I got bored. I had been watching my dad shift the gears from neutral to drive, so I reached over and moved the gear from P for park to N for neutral. The car then started rolling down the hill. I knew enough about driving to put my foot on the brake pedal which stopped the car before it got to the highway. I kept pressure on the brake pedal as long as I could until my leg started getting stiff. I knew that if I took my foot off the brake the car would roll down the hill and crash. I also felt my dad would blame me for any damage done to his car.

My father still had not returned to the car to check on his son. I was nervous, sweating and getting tired. I had an epiphany realizing that all I had to do to keep the car from moving further was to put the gear back into the position of park. I questioned why my father would leave a nine-year-old in his car for about an hour and a half alone. I did not see her but I knew that he was in that house with a woman. As I got older and I began to understand what type of man my father was I knew why he did not care about me sitting in a car alone for a long period of time.

In our house on 20th Street, my mother would sell drinks to make money. My dad would sometimes help her. They had a customer and a friend by the name of Mister Walt. My father from what I remember did not like him. I think it was because Mister Walt had been flirting with my mother. Dad's reaction on one occasion to what he thought was going on was to tell mom he was going to drive out to West Philadelphia. This time he took my sister Lorraine and I with him. He did not drive to West Philly; he only drove a block or two away where he picked up a woman I did not know from her house. We all then rode to Fairmount Park where my sister and I were able to run and play, while he sat in the car with this unnamed person. I was young so I did not know anything about adults cheating or people having affairs.

I was not the type of kid who would go back home and tell my mom that dad had another woman in his car. A couple of years later I found out that the house that the woman came out of was Mister Walt's house, and the lady was Mister Walt's wife. I thought about that situation when I got older and I believe my father was having an affair with Mister Walt's wife.

Mister Walt and a bunch of other guys were always coming over to my house. The one man that I remember always being at our house in the group was Ray Charles. I did not know his real name but he was called by the name of the popular singer because he always wore sunglasses, even at night. It was said that the reason he wore sunglasses was because something happened to his eyes during the war. I left my house one evening and was walking down the street to a store when I passed an alley, where I heard moaning and groaning. My curiosity took control of me as I ventured into the alley. When my eyes adjusted to the dark night, I saw Mister Walt screwing Ray Charles up against a wall. I knew nothing about homosexuality but I soon figured it out.

Across the street from my elementary school was a school for children with emotional problems. The name of that school was Saint Martin. The school had an indoor gym where there were organized basketball teams from the community. There was a coach of one of the teams by the name of Mister Warner.

Sometime later I was in the apartment of a friend when Mister Warner showed up. To my surprise, after being in the apartment awhile he started going around the room giving guys blowjobs. When he got to me, I told him no and waved him away. I heard someone in the background say that I was not into that. I was 12 years old, and knew very little about homosexuals. I now started to notice some of the gay men in the neighborhood.

While riding my bike one day I saw a gay man standing on the side walk. I figured he was gay because of his mannerisms and his feminine style of dress. As I rode pass him, I yelled "Faggot!" He got so mad that he took off his high heels and chased me down the street. I pedaled as fast as I could as I heard him yelling that if he caught my ass, he was going to kill me. He did not catch me. This guy had a friend who was a light complexioned man, while he was a darker skin color. They hung out together. They were tough homosexuals. They knew how to kick ass so nobody messed with them. I stayed away from the area where they hung out after my incident. If I saw them coming down the street I would turn and go the other way. I did not know if that guy remembered what I called him, but I sure did.

My father was four or five years older than my mother. She died at the age of 76. I had a premonition that I too will die at the age of 76. I cannot explain why, it is just a feeling. I was very close to my mother and I miss her all the time. I am comforted in that she saw me become an accomplished singer with a hit making group.

My father died only a few years ago at the age of 102. He was living in Delaware when he passed away. The relationship with my father was distant. He left the family for good when I was nine. While living with us I always felt that he loved my brother Vernon more than he cared for me. He would always say "you are just like your mother!" I did not think that he meant that as a compliment. A strange thing happened on the way to prepare for his funeral. My sister called me and said that we should head to Delaware early and dress our father's body. On the way down to Delaware it was raining hard when the rubber from one of the windshield wipers flew off. We found a Pep Boys automotive store nearby where we replaced the wiper. When we tried to start the car again the battery was dead. I took that as a sign that my father was not ready to go. I felt that this was his way of delaying his departure from this earth.

Chapter 2
"Grateful"

I started school while living at 844 N. 20th Street in North Philadelphia. The name of the elementary school was Bach. It was in the white area of my neighborhood. I lived in the area controlled by a gang named the Morocco's. Their territory covered approximately from Fairmount Ave to Broad Street and Girard and Corinthian Avenues to Broad Street. My problem now was that I lived in the Morocco's territory, but my elementary school was in an area controlled by a white gang. I had to be creative everyday traveling back and forth to school. Bach Elementary School was where I first met Keith Beaton who was to become a member of Blue Magic. At the time we met we had no idea that someday we would be members in a successful singing group.

We met by chance one day when I was sent to the school nurses office to take a cube of medicine which prevented polio. All the children in school received the same medicine but for some reason I missed getting the medicine with my class. While I was sitting in the nurse's office alone, another little boy came into the office and took a seat. The one thing I remember about him during this first encounter was that he looked mad. We did not speak but I thought well at least now I am not sitting here by myself. It just so happened that we ended up being in the same fourth, fifth· and sixth grade classes. We were never close friends during that time other than to speak to each other. As fate would have it my brother

Vernon was also in our elementary school at that time. Later in life I thought back and felt the stars were aligning then for Blue Magic. I felt that even then we were destined to be together.

Sometime later I was a proud safety crossing guard on the corner of Corinthian Ave and Parrish Street. This was my first experience with having some authority as I helped little children and my classmates cross the busy street to our school. Once while at my post I noticed this girl coming down the street holding the hand of a little boy who turned out to be her brother. What I thought was odd about this little boy was that he appeared to have a shadow over his lip which turned out to be a mustache. He was only five or six years old. I had never seen anything like that on a kid his age. He also looked mean like he did not want to go to school. This little boy with the mustache turned out to be Richard Pratt who would also become a member of Blue Magic.

Like many of my contemporaries Vernon and I sang in the choir at the New Welcome Baptist Church which was and still is located at 20th and Parrish Streets. I used to listen to the radio and sing along to the songs of The Five Stair Steps, The Mad Lads, The O J' s, The Dells. and sometime later the Topics with lead singer Ted Mills. I never thought seriously about music until I took a music course in the 8th grade. The teacher asked each student to sing. When I completed singing her response was," You really can sing!" That was the first time I realized that I could carry a tune. I had a friend who was one of the coolest guys I knew. I hung out with him all the time. I remember one time at a dance when we were in the

7th grade, he jumped up on the stage and started lip singing while gyrating across the stage. The girls watching him went wild. Watching that I thought to myself that I wanted those types of accolades. That was my first taste of what it must be like to be a performer. Although I liked what I saw I did not think that I had the confidence to get up on the stage in front of all those people.

During my early years I felt that I also had my first experience with racism. My 3rd grade teacher was named Miss Wormsley. Because of how she treated me I will never forget her name. Three boys and two girls in my class were given permission to go to the water fountain outside of the classroom. While in the hallway two of the boys were cursing. I was just standing there waiting my turn at the water fountain, not saying a word. When the group went back into the classroom the girls told the teacher about the profanity used by the boys outside of the classroom. Miss Wormsley asked me why I was cursing during my water break. I told her that I was not cursing and after denying it for a second time she yelled at me" Do not lie to me!" She then slapped me hard in the face. Following the slap, she made me and the other two boys stand in front of the class with soapy wash clothes in our mouths. I felt that she did this to us because we were black. I do not think she would have done that to little white boys. She slapped me for no reason, even after I told the truth. I was a little black boy so this white teacher assumed that I must have lied.

There was another time when I got to high school where I thought racism applied. I was told by an old white teacher that I should take courses that would allow me to develop a trade such as carpentry. I was a good student but that did not matter to him. I followed his suggestion because I did not know any better. I did not have any adults in my life who could advise me. My mother was an uneducated woman and my father was not around. My brother Vernon, however, did not listen to those suggestions; so, he took college preparatory courses.

At the age of fifteen there was a protest near my home. The protest was because the whites only Girard College was not allowing Black students to attend the school. Invited to speak at the protest was a dynamic speaker who I found out later was Doctor Martin Luther King Jr. I must admit at that time that I knew nothing about Dr. King. During that time period, I must admit that I knew very little about the civil rights movement. I knew nothing about civil right icons such as James Meredith, Medgar Evers, or Rosa Parks. Those people or the movement was not discussed in my household.

When the protest was over the police started yelling at the crowd to disperse. When we did not move as fast as they would have liked they began pushing and shoving. I watched a motorcycle cop ride just about over a pregnant black woman. Another police officer saw me witness this terrible action and began to chase me down the street. I knew the area well, he did not. I avoided capture by running through back alleys and over fences.

There was a girl in my neighborhood by the name of Toni. She would organize protests concerning Girard College. I guess that you would have called her a political activist. She was heavily involved in the black power movement. She was a light skinned girl who would not give me the time of day. She told me once that she did not like me because my nose and lips were too big, and the color of my skin was too dark. So much for black power. One day she was kidnapped. She was missing for about a week. While the police supposedly searched for her, I remember seeing a police car in front of her house everyday during the investigations. She eventually was dropped off in front of her house. During her time in captivity, she was injected with heroin and now was addicted. I never knew who kidnapped her or why. Rumor had it that it was because of her activist work. She never really recovered from her addiction problem. She eventually overdosed and died, at around seventeen years old.

In my neighborhood the gangs controlled the streets. I had to fight every day. I had to defend myself so often that I thought everyone everywhere had the same experiences. I thought it had to be the norm, since it was happening to me. We were poor, so I had no exposure to anything outside of my own environment. I could not conceive that people lived another way.

One Saturday my mother gave my brother and I money to go to the local movie theatre. It was not that far from our home but it was in Morocco Territory. A gang member saw us and said that we looked like we were going somewhere. He asked us if we had any money? He then came up to me. In response to his invading my private space I put my hands up to defend myself. He then told me to put my hands down. Once I complied, he put his hand in my pocket and took my damn money. He then walked away without saying a word. I knew that the Morocco gang controlled the area so it was the right thing to do to give him what he wanted.

In my neighborhood there were many different gangs. There was the Seybert Street Gang, The 16th and Wallace Street Gang, and the 12th and Popular Street Gang. Most of these Gangs took their names from the streets that they lived on. The gang that controlled where I lived was call the Morocco gang. I was told that the Morocco's were originally a local baseball team. Gangs started to invade their neighborhood. Subsequently they ended up fighting these groups. They decided now to call themselves the Morocco gang. There was probably about two hundred members in the gang when I lived in their territory. They were labeled by age. There was the Old Heads, the Juniors, and the Midget Morocco. The Midget Morocco gang was the youngest members. Although my mother did not want us to join a gang, Vernon decided to become a Morocco.

My mother and I were sitting in the living room one evening when Vernon at the age of thirteen came running into the house, fell on the floor and started vomiting wine. Mom put a bucket under his head as he vomited in the bucket. He was so drunk that his head fell into the vomit in the bucket. I was laughing at him the whole time. I knew that to join the gang my brother had to drink down a quart of wine. What mom and I witnessed was the result of his initiation. He also fried his hair with a chemical to straighten it to look like the hair of white men. It was called "processed hair style." Unfortunately, too many of us were doing that to ourselves at that time. My mother tried to wash it out without any success. She realized that it would have to grow out or be cut off. Vernon had to take his 6th grade graduation pictures with that processed hair. My mother made him get out of the game.

Another incident happened when I first got to high school. My mother bought Vernon and I leather coats. Leather coats at that time were a status symbol, like Air Jordan's are to kids today. A friend of mine approached me at school and told me that members of a street gang had my brother hemmed up in a corner and were going to take his leather coat. He explained to the group that "he was the brother of his friend, and asked them to leave him alone, which they did.

I was now learning how to deal in the world in which we lived. You do not have to act in physical ways, you can use your brain to navigate through situations. My survival was more mental than physical. I was not a gang member but I used to hang out with the leader of the Morocco gang. His name was Kilroy. He never put pressure on me to join the gang. He was a cool dude, and we became good friends. To be the leader of the gang you had to fight and beat up the other top members. Big Don, who was the brother of Blue Magic member Keith Beaton, was the next member to lead that gang.

As a result of being poor, I remember waking up one morning and seeing blood spots all over my sheets. I showed my mother the bloody sheets and she then pulled up the mattress. Under the mattress I saw thousands of tiny black bugs. I knew nothing about bed bugs. My mom just sprayed down the bed, and then I went back to sleeping on it. I had no choice. We did not have the money to replace the mattress. We also had to share our living quarters with mice and rats. I had a cat named Mary Ann. She was a fierce hunter. When I woke up in the morning, I saw feet and tails from the rodents she killed. We were too poor to buy cat food, so her nightly hunts filled her belly. We did not have air conditioning. There was a fan, but mom got that at night. All we could do was raise our bedroom windows and hope for an occasional breeze. The only drawback to sleeping with the windows open was that there was no screen to keep out the mosquitos. I was living in a world of hell! Bed bugs and mosquitos biting me while mice partied around my bed on the floor. We did not care; it was what we got used too. The only luxury item I remember us having was a television. My father brought one home. I was instantly fascinated by this box where I saw people moving around inside. We had an ice box not a refrigerator. When my mother went shopping, I had to take my wagon to the corner store and pick up a block of ice.

Around thirteen or fourteen years old I decided that I wanted to make some money of my own, so I got myself a shoe shine box. I would go to downtown Philly and shine the shoes of the white men on the street. One evening when I returned home, I had a pocket full of money after a successful day of work. Before I reached the sanctuary of my home, I ran into a Morocco who asked me for some money. I lied and told him that I did not have any. That boy then slapped me in the face so hard that I started crying. Taking that slap was worth, because I was successful in getting home with my money.

Another time I went to the store to buy some candy. When I came out of the store there was a Morocco that I had to walk pass. He was sucking on a lemon, and as I walked by him, he squirted the lemon juice in my eyes for no apparent reason other than to be cruel. Then there was the time when I was in the park with my friends planning to play basketball when a Morocco approached us and asked us if we wanted a sandwich? I was hungry so I answered yes. When I opened the sandwich to see what was inside, I found a dead mouse in between the lettuce, tomatoes and mayonnaise. I thought to myself, what type of individual would think up something as evil as that? I hated to think what would have happen to me if I had not looked inside that sandwich.

There was another guy in my neighborhood whose nickname was" Crazy." That was the appropriate name for him because he was bad. He joined the Morocco's as soon as he moved in to the neighborhood. One day we got word of some of his antics. Crazy, was dressed in complete Indian attire including Indian headdress with feathers. It was reported that he was running around the streets shooting people in the back with his bow and arrows. The arrows were real. That mad man and I never got along.

There was another maniac I had to constantly deal with. I do not remember his name, but for whatever reason he just did not like me. One day I came out of a classroom in the fourth grade and passed him in the hall. He looked at me and out of nowhere, with a twisted face, said "I do not like you. You look like a girl!" Another time he caught me on the playground during recess and told me that he was going to kick my ass. I tried to avoid fights but I would fight to defend myself. If I had to fight I would. This was one of those occasions. I hit him so hard that he said to me "Why are you hitting me so hard?" When he said that I realized that he was not a bully, he was a punk. Coming to that conclusion I thought to myself I am really going to mess him up, which I did. I realized sometime later in my development that many bullies were just like him. They were punks too. I often wondered what happened to him.

Then there was my friend that we all called Skip. The first time I brought him to our house after he left my mother asked me not to hang out with him. I asked her why and she answered that there was something wrong with him. I was 16, what did my mother know, so I started hanging out with him. Our first adventure happened when one day Skip decided that he wanted some money because he had none. He told me that my old friend from elementary school, father was gay. I had met this man previously and thought that he was a nice guy. Skip told me that he was going to get some money from this man. We then went to this dingy hotel which could have been a boarding house. The hallways were dark but there was just enough light to see. Skip asked me to wait at the end of one of the halls. He then walked down the hall and was met by the man he was seeking, as he was coming out of a room. They spoke for a second and then went into a room across the hall. My curiosity caused me to walk down the hall closer to the room. I heard Skip through the door ask the man for some money which he then replied that he did not have any! The next thing I heard was a slap followed by a scream. The room then got silent. I could not hear what was going on in the room after that but I thought they were having sex. Several minutes later Skip came out of the room with some money.

The next adventure with Skip happened around 15th and Fairmount Ave where there was a Chinese Cleaners with a big open glass window in the front of the building. Anyone walking by could look in to the store. Skip had that itch for money that he had to scratch. He did not care, who might see him. He went into the store, leaped over the counter, punched the owner in the face and demanded money. The poor man told him he did not have any. Skip smacked the man again and then opened the cash register taking what money was there. I just stood outside and watched. Skip just committed a strong-arm robbery that I witnessed.

There was a store on 15th Avenue by the name of" Pop's." Fifteenth Avenue was the dividing line between the black and white neighborhoods. Pops was on the white side of the street. An old white couple came out of the store and were walking down the street arm in arm when Skip decided that he was going to snatch the old woman's purse. That is exactly what he did. As he grabbed for her purse the old woman hung on tightly and was dragged down the block until she let go. Her husband was so old he could not really help. Skip ran off with the purse with me following. We went to my mother's house. When we opened the pocketbook, there was only about six dollars inside. This was clearly predatory behavior and I was involved. We changed our clothes before going back outside figuring that the description of the robbers were two black men wearing certain clothes. We then went up to 20th and Popular Streets and hung out on the corner. While there we saw a police car pass by with the old couple in the back seat looking for us. They looked at everyone on the corner and then moved on. The clothes change must have worked.

One day I went to a discount clothing store with my mother and Skip. While there I saw a suit that I thought was nice. I really liked it. I put the suit back on the rack and then told the sales person that I wanted the suit and that I would come back and get it. The sales person agreed to put the suit up for me. When I got back to my home Skip pulled the suit out from under his clothes. He had gone into the dressing room and stuffed the suit along with some other clothes under what he was wearing. In those days it was much easier to steal from those types of discount stores. To say that I was pissed off is being kind. "Didn't you see that I wanted that suit?" I yelled at him! To top it off he would not sell it to me. I do not think that he was there when I said that I liked the suit, but the larceny in his heart told him to steal it. At least we both had the same taste in clothes.

Skip had an older brother. He had a job and was saving up money to take his girlfriend to his senior prom. Skip found out about his brother's bank account, and consequently would go to the bank sign his brother's name and withdraw money from the account. I was with him on some of those occasions so I saw him do it. When his sibling was ready to make his withdrawal for the prom, he found out all his money was gone. He was shown the signature card on the withdrawals and he knew it was Skip. He went home after this shocking discovery and beat Skip's ass. I witnessed the ass kicking. I felt bad for his brother and a bit guilty. I knew what Skip was doing. I should have told his brother.

I had been lucky so far hanging out with Skip while he was involved in larcenous behavior. My luck was about to come to an end. Skip had a cashmere coat that he spilled something on. It left a stain that could not be removed. He consequently decided that he now wanted to replace the coat. We went the John Wanamaker department store in search of a new one. Vernon was with us this time. We located the men's coat department where Skip started trying on coats. I was holding his old coat. My brother was left by the escalator leading out of the building as a lookout. Skip tried on a coat and said I do not like this one. He took the coat off and handed it to me. We then went to another coat area where he tried on another coat. I was now holding two coats. He once again said that he did not see anything that he liked. By now I had taken the tags off the new coat and placed them on the dirty coat. He then hung the two coats back on the rack one of which was his old coat. We did not know it but we were being watched by security from behind a one-way mirror. When we turned to leave the store, we noticed that Vernon was gone. Seconds later we were approached by store security and taken into custody. We were held until the police came. We were then taken to the Round House, which was the local Philadelphia jail. While being processed at the Round House an officer asked me my age. When I told him that I was sixteen he looked at me again and said I looked like I was twenty-four. All my friends purposely dressed and tried to look older so that we could hang out in the bars in my neighborhood. I was in a cell by myself for about 5 hours. During that time, I heard things that made me realize that I never wanted to go to jail again. I also thought about my mother's previous warning to not associate with Skip.

I figured that Vernon had gone home and told my mother what happened. I found out after she came an got me that he never told her about the incident. When I arrived back home Vernon told me that when he spotted security he left. I suspect that I never went to court on that case because the store did not press charges and they got their merchandise back. Jail scared me enough that I knew it was time to leave Skip alone. My mother was right. I should have listened to her when she warned me about him. Keith Beaton told me some time ago he was in West Philadelphia when he heard someone call his name. He did not recognize the guy until he identified himself. It was Skip. He had a scraggly beard, and unkept hair. Keith said that he looked like a bum. I guess his life had come full circle. Skip died shortly after that Keith sighting.

The other problem that most black men had to deal with in my ghetto was of course the police. I was no exception. Being poor and black automatically made me a target. I remember one occasion while walking down the street one summer, when the police stopped me. I happened to be wearing a long sleeve shirt at the time. A police officer jumped out of his car and forcefully told to me to get up against the wall. I anxiously asked him what did I do? He responded by telling me to pull up the sleeves on my shirt. He examined my arms looking for track marks. He did not find any. He then told his partner" He's Alright!" They obviously profiled me as a junkie. I was sixteen years old and had not had any experience with the illicit drug use beyond marijuana, so I did not understand why I was stopped. They gave me no explanation for the stop or apology for their behavior.

I attended Benjamin Franklin High School. The gang that claimed control of that area was the 12th and Popular Street Gang. I had to use my brains, in order to survive since I was not a member of any gang. As in most gang hierarchies they had members of that group who were called "Old Heads." They were older gang members who had graduated from Ben Franklin or just dropped out of school. When I entered the school in the 10th grade, they told the younger active gang members not to mess with me. They saved me and although I never understood why or what was going on, I was thankful. Subsequently I used my street smarts, and made friends, while in school with some of the top members of the other gangs. One day the 12th and Popular Street Gang surrounded the school and covered all the entrances and exits. They would ask everyone entering or leaving the school "Where you from?" Giving the wrong answer would result in getting your ass kicked. Vernon and another one of our friends chose not to go to school. I, however, walked right through the gang and into the school, without any problems.

When I was attending Ben Franklin High most of the teachers were white. As I look back on it, their attitudes and behavior, I believe, suggested they were only there to get a pay check. I do not believe most of them had their hearts in teaching us black kids. I did have one teacher by the name of Mister Davis that I liked. He taught math. It was because of him that I developed a love of math. If you had a math problem that you did not understand he would sit with you individually until you got it. He was the nicest teacher that I can remember having during my whole high school experience. He made an impression on me because he would take time with me and other students, and defend us if necessary. Some of the white teachers would teach you something in the subject they taught one time, and if you did not understand what was taught you were on your own. They made me think that they did not care whether you passed or failed. During a class session one of the teachers thought he was giving the class hygiene lessons by telling the class that soap and water would keep us clean, suggesting that we had poor hygiene. That was humiliating. I felt that they sometimes treated us like we were animals. Mister Davis, who was black was not like that. He was the only black teacher that I had the whole time I was in school, that I felt cared.

In 1968 I graduated from high school. It was right in the middle of the Vietnam War. It was right after graduation that I received a notice from the draft board to report for a physical. During the physical I was asked if I could I take orders. My response to the question was "No I don't even take orders from my parents!" I was then told that I needed to be seen by a psychiatrist. I went home and delivered that message to my parents. On Girard Avenue, not that far from my home, there was a psychiatrist's office. My mother took me to his office. When I

went into the room to talk, I noticed that once I closed the door behind me, I could not see the door anymore. I quickly realized that the room was full of illusions. We talked for quite a while bantering back and forth. The doctor finally said that he thought I was 4F. He then gave me a letter to take back to the draft board. Within a couple weeks I received another letter to report down to 30th Street train Station. When I arrived, I saw all these guys with bags and suit cases. I had to explain that I was there only to present a letter from a psychiatrist stating that I was 4F. I was told that the letter had to be presented to the military psychiatrist. I then proceeded to their psychiatrist's office. He looked at the letter and said "this is a friend of mine; it is O K; you are 4F."

I did not want to go into the army and did not want to go to Vietnam. One of my friends came back from Vietnam and, ended up a resident in a Sanatorium. He was shell shocked and he never recovered. Another person I knew from the neighborhood who went by the name of Beach Comer came home in a casket. Beach Comer was a Morocco. I was not going to Vietnam. I felt no such loyalty to America after the things that I experienced and witnessed here at home. Keith wanted to go but had bad eye sight. Vernon was also planning on joining. The draft lottery in 1970 changed Vernon's mind.

His draft lottery number was so high that he would never be called to serve. In subsequent years I learned that my high school lost more of its former students in Vietnam than any other high school in Philadelphia.

My brother and I Had our own bond. Vernon bought a 1963 Oldsmobile Electra 225. The slang name for that car was "Deuce and a Quarter." One morning we woke up to find out that someone had stolen his car. We got into my mother's car and began searching for my brother's car. Although guns were not really that widely available, I had a starter pistol. I brought it along in case we contacted the thieves. I hoped that I could use it to scare them. As bad luck would happen while we were searching for the car, we got stopped by the police. When this happened, I shoved the gun way up in a corner under the front seat. They made us get out of the car, subsequently searching the vehicle. They took so long searching the car I started sweating. While they were searching, I thought to myself how stupid it was of me to bring the pistol. Trying to be tough did not matter now. Scaring the car thief did not matter now. Fortunately for me they did not find the weapon. I do not know why they did not find the gun but I was sure glad that they did not. They let us go.

My brother Vernon's experiences, in our teens, although only a year younger was different from mine. Keith, Vernon, a few other guys, and myself went to a local bar one evening. We were all around sixteen and seventeen years old. We tried to dress older by wearing long coats and hats. Nobody back then bothered to check identification. The bar tenders knew we were young but they left us alone. On this particular night an "old head" from the Morocco's was in the bar. In this packed bar he gets into an argument with another patron. They decided to take the argument outside. Vernon went along to watch, while the rest of us kept our seats at the bar. As soon as they got outside according to Vernon, the patron shot the man he was arguing with in the head and killed him. Vernon witnessed the whole incident. He did not seem to phased by the blood and brains scattered on the side walk. It was disturbing to me. I had never seen anyone shot before. I always tried to avoid situations that could end in that type of result. We did not go back to that bar for a while after that murder.

Sometime later Keith, another friend and I decided to return there thinking that the smoke had cleared. Why did we do that? While in the bar two guys approached us from the 15th street and Wallace gang. They knew that Keith's brother Big Don was the leader of the Morocco gang. They wanted to fight him, so they did what they could to push him in that direction. When we left the Bar Keith tried to avoid the fight with one of the guys but he ended up doing what he had to do. He beat the guy up as he picked him up and slammed him down on a car hood. I was surprise because I had never seen Keith that angry. He was not that type of person.

Chapter 3
"Tear It Down"

There was a store that made the best Philly cheese steaks in the area. The only problem was that it was in the white section of the neighborhood. Some of my friends and myself usually walked to this hoagie and steak shop. If you do not know what a hoagie is it is made up of all types of cold cut meats such as salami, bologna, lettuce, tomatoes, onions, and cheese on a long roll. This group of my friends all refused to join the Morocco gang. We formed our own gang or club that we called 2-0-P which meant 20th and Popular. We were respected in our neighborhood even by the Morocco gang. That respect came after us fighting members of the gang and beating them up. The gang member took our tough stance back to other gang members and we were then left alone.

On one occasion while walking to the steak shop a white boy jumped out of the bushes with an axe and swung it at my head missing me by inches. The only reason he did not try again was because he saw a cop car coming up the block. On another occasion we were on our way to get some steak sandwiches when we were confronted by a bunch of white guys again. One of my friends started fighting one of them. He was kicking this guy's ass when we heard someone yell "run!" There were just too many white guys for us to fight and win, so we got the hell out of the area.

When my friends and I were going to Bates Elementary which was in the white neighborhood, there was a white guy we called "Red" because he had red hair. He was older and bigger than most of us. He tormented us every time he saw one of us black kids while we were on our way to school. He would approach us and either push us down or smack us upside the head. We hated him. Years later as teenagers we found out that the dummy had a grandmother who lived in our section of the neighborhood. At one point the area where I lived was probably all white. White flight took place, but she did not. She probably did not have anywhere else to go that she could afford, so she stayed. Keith first saw him in our area and discovered he was visiting his grandmother. He told his brother Don who was a member of the Morocco gang. The gang caught Red, coming from a visit and beat his ass. I never saw Red in my neighborhood again.

My friends and I were not angels. While in Junior High School a few friends and I used to roam around the white neighborhood looking for white boys to beat up. One day we ran into one who was not afraid to fight. He was beating my friend's ass so bad that my best friend at the time stepped in to save him. We then heard an old woman yell from her window that she was going to call the cops. That was our signal to leave. We never let my friend live down his ass kicking. He picked the wrong white boy to mess with.

When my father left, my mother began partially supporting the family by organizing card games in a second-floor apartment, where one of her friends lived. Poker was the main game played. In Philadelphia at that time, gambling was illegal. The first thing that I noticed about my mother's friend was that her upper lip was missing. It was not funny, but it was funny to me. I found out that her boyfriend got pissed off with her about something she said one time and shoved a beer bottle in her mouth breaking her teeth and cutting off her lip. I thought that she must have been a beautiful woman before she lost her lip. What was even more amazing to me was that after that incident they stayed together.

The police used to bust in and arrest everyone including my mother and her friend. The cops raided the games so often that my mother's picture was posted on the wall in the local police precinct. When I saw her picture on the wall in the police station, I realized how often she must have been busted. It was embarrassing, when some of my friends pointed out that they saw the picture. My mother was the top numbers banker in North Philadelphia for many years. Because of her continued activity on such a high level she was always the target of the police. She was in and out of jail for short periods of time because her activities were well known to law enforcement. I do remember one time during one of the poker games there was a big fight and money was flying everywhere including out of the windows. Vernon and I ran into the hallway and picked up as much money as we could.

Being a Numbers Banker, was against the law. Gambling was against the law. My mother did these things however, to feed her family. She was a strong black woman.

I had a few of what I thought were near death experiences during my life. One of those experiences happened when Vernon and I found a bullet on the street. I took the bullet and threw in into a fire to see what would happen. Suddenly I heard a big pop. The bullet shot out of the fire hit a nearby wooden fence. A piece of wood from that fence dislodged and hit me in the chest. I looked down at my chest and saw blood. Opening my shirt, I was relieved when I found out that it was not the bullet but a piece of wood from the fire. This to me was a brush with death. It could have been the bullet that hit me in the chest, as I watched it move around in the flame. I could have died!

On another occasion at the age of sixteen, I started dating this beautiful girl. She lived in a section of Philadelphia called Tioga. This area was fascinating to me because the people lived in one family attached row homes, many with front porches. The area I lived in was surrounded by Projects and houses that were broken up into apartments. On many streets if the front windows to the house were open you could look in them from the sidewalk and see clear back to the kitchen. I did not know much about this young lady but I did not care because she looked good. I just remember being in love with her. My first time going to visit her at home, what I did not know was that her brother was the leader of the 23rd and Venango Streets Gang. The first thing she did when I entered her house was to introduce me to her brother. All the top members in the gang happened to be sitting in the living room. At first, I was intimidated, while trying to be cool. I then thought to myself Hell what am I scare of? I am from the Morocco territory! I am tough and can handle this. While I was sitting on the living room sofa with these gang members, a call came in that a rival gang was seen in the Venango Street area. The members of the gang all rushed out of the house. Trying to prove myself to my new girlfriend and her brother, I went out into the street with them. Back then there were very few fights where guns were involved. A gang member may use a belt, a bat, or a car radio antenna that you ripped off a car but, guns were rare. When we saw the rival gang down the street, I jumped out in front of the crowd. The sun was going down and in the shadows of the gray sky we saw the interlopers at a distance. We all started yelling "let's fight!" I happened to be standing right next to a big tree. I suddenly heard a loud pop and something hit the tree next to me. I quickly realized that it was a bullet from a gun that was aimed at me. Once someone fired a gun at us we all ran like hell. Thinking back on that incident some years later I thought that was another near-death experience for me.

Shortly after that incident I was walking down the street with my new love interest when a guy bumped me as I passed him. We had a few words which resulted in a fist fight. I lost the fight. The next day my lady friend broke my heart by terminating our relationship. I was in love with her. I did not understand what I did and she gave me no explanation.

Some years later I thought about that incident and consequently believe that her brother set the fight up to see if I was tough. I guess because I lost the fight, I was not tough enough for his sister.

Then there was the time I went out to a lake with my brother and some friends where we rented a canoe. Everyone on the boat including my brother Vernon could swim; everyone except me. When we got out in the middle of the lake everyone jumped into the water. My friend David stayed in the boat because he was doing the paddling. I looked around and saw little white kids in the water. Not really thinking, I decided to join everyone, who appeared to be having such a good time. The next thing I remember was that the water was over my head. All I saw when I opened my eyes was muddy water. As luck would have it when I jumped into the water, I was fortunate enough to have kept one hand holding onto one side of the boat. That hand enabled me to spring my body back into the boat. There was no doubt that if I had not had my hand on the side of the boat I might have drowned. None of my friends swam well enough to have probably saved me. Over the years my brushes with death seemed to have come more frequently than for most of the people I knew.

My Blue Magic member Keith Beaton and I knew each other through elementary and junior high school. While I went to Benjamin Franklin High School, Keith was sent by his parents to Dobbins High School. He could not go to Franklin, because his brother ran the Morocco gang. Going to a school where there were many gangs interacting could very well have caused his death. We got back together after high school.

We became good friends again after high school. His situation at the time was less than stellar. He had a three-story house to himself. His father bought the house as income property. All Keith had to do was pay the monthly bills, from the money his father sent home which he failed to do. Keith's mother passed away when he was in junior high school. His father was a merchant marine so he was basically on his own.

When the house was foreclosed on, he subsequently became homeless. .

Keith and I went to the Blue Horizon Ballroom for what was called at the time a Cabaret. This was the type party where everyone brought their own bottles of liquor. Keith and I brought a fifth of liquor and while sitting at a table in the party we drank most of it. We were waiting for my friend Skip to join us. I got so drunk that the band who was playing appeared to be upside down. I knew for a fact now that I was" tore up from the neck up." Skip brought another fifth of liquor with him when he arrived. I told both of my friends that I was drunk and had enough. I decided to leave the party and go see my girlfriend who was at her grandmother's house. I stumbled all the way down Broad Street bumping into buildings, along the way. I was lucky that the cops did not see me. I did make it to grandmother's home. The next day I woke up and tried unsuccessfully to contact Keith. Another day passed and I still had not heard from him so I went to where he was living and he was not there. On day three he showed up at my door and told me why he had been missing. Apparently after leaving the party Skip volunteered to drive Keith's girlfriend home in this small foreign car that he owned. Somewhere along the road after dropping her off they had an accident-causing Keith to be thrown from the car. I asked him then what happened? He answered that he did not know. He said the police took him to the local precinct and tried to charge him with drunk driving. While in custody they took him to hospital where he <u>was</u> treated for a broken leg. Keith did not know what happened to Skip. A week later Skip showed up. He explained that while driving he skidded on something in the road as he saw Keith get ejected from the car. He said that the car then went over an embankment and landed in some bushes after which he lost consciousness. Skip figured he had been in the car for a week before he regained consciousness. I thought to myself after hearing his story that Skip was already crazy so the last thing, he needed was further head trauma.

I eventually asked my mother could Keith move in with us because of his continued hard times. Upon her approval that is what he did. That was when the two of us started singing together.

Keith had a tumultuous life. He lived with his mother until her death. Being a merchant marine his father did not spend much time at home. He had two brothers and one sister. They were Big Don, his sister Merlin, and his brother Toe, short for his nickname Tokay. Tokay was a cheap wine that we drank. Toe's real name was Gregory. He got that name after drinking a half gallon of Tokay wine as his initiation to join the Morocco's gang. I was not sure how long his siblings lived in the home. When his mother died his father continued sending his money home to Keith who was only fifteen years old. He was expected to take care of the house. Very few fifteen year olds can take care of such a task. Keith was no exception. The water, gas and electric were eventually cut off. The house gradually deteriorated. He had no money because the money that was sent home, he spent on things that he did not need. He had no finances to ride public transportation. Since he did not have any money, he had to run from 19ᵗʰ and Popular Streets to Dobbins High school. The distance from his residence to school was quite a long way. He had to be creative in order to avoid the different gangs.

When his father came home and saw how the house had deteriorated, rather than fix it up he bought another house at 72nd and Walnut Streets. I thought his father was a very nice guy. He always had stories about his travels. I remember him telling us that in one country that he visited it was so dangerous that he had to take his money into the shower with him so it would not get stolen.

During a severe snow storm one year, the streets of course were covered. Keith's brother Toe drove down his block, and stopped his car in the middle of the small street, where he decided to shovel out a space to park. Another car pulled up behind him and the driver wanted him to move his car so that he could pass. If Toe moved his car, he would have to drive all the way around the block to get back to the spot he had almost completely shoveled. Doing that could possibly mean that he would lose the spot he had shoveled, so he refused to move. The driver of the other car got out and approached Toe. What he did not realize was that this man was carrying a butcher knife, which after a brief argument, he used to stab Toe in the chest. Toe staggered up to his front door. Keith opened the door after hearing his brother knocking. When he opened the door, Toe fell into his arms. Keith told me that before he died a large splash of blood shot out of his chest and hit the wall.

On another sad occasion when Keith came home from

one of our road trips, he entered the house where he lived with his father. He found his father, who had retired dead. His father's body was so swollen that it suggested that he had been dead for at least three days.

We were on another road trip, when we got back home, I received a phone call from Keith. "Wendell, I just came in the house and found Don dead on the floor!" It took a minute to process what he had just told me. I realized then that he was the first person in our singing group to see four of his family members pass away. That was a bunch of traumatic experiences for anyone to have to deal with. I admired Keith because even after those negative experiences he kept moving on.

CHAPTER 4
"WELCOME TO THE CLUB"

I believe that if Keith had not moved in with me, and we started singing together, there would have never been the inception of Blue Magic. We subsequently recruited a third member, Richard "Rick" Pratt, and another guy to sing with us, in the beginning. We wanted Vernon to join the group but he was not interested. He was into girls, and he had a job. He looked down on us at that time. He thought that singing was beneath him. He was right about one thing. Keith and I were unemployed and not looking for work. He embarrassed me to the point that I decided to get a job. I went to work for a company named Bookbinders. My job there was restoring old books. Once I got to know the people that I worked with, I was able to get Keith a job. He did not last long there. I enjoyed working there. It did put some money in my pocket. It was so great that I could leave for three weeks to a month, come back, and tell the supervisor Chuck that I wanted to work again. He would just tell me to go and sign in. Great job! It broke my heart when the business moved so far away that I had to take a couple of buses to get there. I was spoiled. Where the company was originally located, I could walk to work. While working there I told one my coworker's that one day I was going to be a star. I told him that when I do, I am going to come back and show them what I forecasted.

When success happened, I went back to the company in a limousine. I walked inside of the building with pride and showed my old coworkers one of the results of my fame. I did not know if I was going to be successful when I made that prognostication, but I made the prediction anyway. I just felt that someday I would be famous.

We were finally able to perform at a local show. A couple of hours before going on stage, we were introduced to and given a drug called Dexedrine, street name "Desi." Medically Dexedrine is used to treat attention deficit problems with hyperactivity. It was a mild stimulant. When we got on stage are recruited member was a mess. I did not know if it was the drugs or he had stage fright. He forgot the words to the song, so Keith and I had to cover for him. We knew after that performance that we needed to replace him. We were lucky because Vernon saw our show and realized we were serious. It did not take much convincing now for him to join the group. We now called our group SHADES OF LOVE. We gave ourselves that name because we all were different shades of black.

There was another group named Blue Magic at that time. They were much older guys. It was rumored that the original group got their name from the infamous New York drug dealer Frank Lucas, who called the packages of heroin he put out on the street Blue Magic.

Before becoming Blue Magic, The Shades of Love had some experiences of their own. In downtown Philadelphia there was a Radio Shack that had a small stage. The manager of the store was named Leroy Jones. He was a very nice guy. One day while in the store we decided to get up on the stage and sing to the music played in the store. Suddenly, the store filled up with customers not to buy anything, but to listen to us and watch our choreography. Leroy became our first manager. He took the group to places that we had never been. We were eighteen and nineteen-year-old young men from the ghetto. We had little exposure beyond our own immediate environment. I remember him taking us to this Seafood restaurant in South Philadelphia called Snookey's. We had lobsters for the first time. The closest delicacy we had eaten before hanging out with Leroy was Philly cheese steaks. Snookey's was a plush upscale Restaurant. Leroy ordered everything for us on our maiden voyage to the restaurant. Once we became successful, we often went back there to dine. I always remembered my first time there.

Leroy bought us our first sound system. He invited us to his home in New Jersey. When there we practiced singing and choreography. He introduced us to this drug called" Tac." I did not know what it was but I tried it anyway. Once I snorted it, I found that it burned the hell out of my nose. Then I started hallucinating. He set up a show for us to perform at the Blue Horizon Ballroom on Broad Street in Philadelphia. He bought us outfits which consisted of white Jump suits, with yellow shirts and white hats. He had this idea for our group to also wear masks. Keith shot that idea down. When it was time to perform on the show featuring the masks they could not be found. I believe to this day that Keith was responsible for making them disappear, even though he never admitted it.

Blue Magic members Keith Beaton, Richard Pratt, Vernon Sawyer and myself used to go down into my mother's basement, and listen to different artists sing songs on the radio. Subsequently, we learned how to sing the ones that we liked. There was a group we heard on the radio by the name of the Toppiks. We loved the way they sung. Their lead singer was named Ted Mills. We also liked to smoke marijuana while rehearsing. Like most weed smokers we had our own regular dealer. One day we were over at his house smoking and buying some weed, when the subject turned to how much we enjoyed the music of the Toppiks and Ted Mills. He told us that he knew Ted Mills personally. I asked him to please call us the next time Ted came over his house to visit, which he did. When we got the call we rushed over to his home. We were introduced to Ted. We sang for him, on this first meeting. He then told us that he liked our performance. We then asked him if he would help us in advancing our careers. He in turn told us that he wanted to introduce us to his management company. Ted was a music major at Temple University at the time so not to long after our meeting he took us to the school where he played, the songs "Spell, What's Come Over Me, and Tear it Down."

Ted kept his promise and introduced us to his management company WMOT. We sung for them and were told that they really liked what they heard. Hearing our vocal renditions, they offered, our group a contract. We did not know anything about contracts, nor were we expecting to be offered one. They gave us the contract that day and told us to take it home and look it over. We rode to the meeting in Vernon's car so now on the way home with the contract, we were trying to figure out our next move. We were just young guys from the ghetto. We did not know how to proceed. There was a man who lived across the street from my mother who used to give Keith piano lessons. I never knew before that day that Keith had ever taken any lessons. His name was Mister Covington. Since he was the only person, we knew with any experience in the music business that we could trust, we asked him to examine the contract. Mister Covington obliged us by examining the contract and then told us that he thought it was a "slave contract." He pointed out that everything we were promised on the front end of the contract that they take back on the back pages of the contract. He suggested that we not sign it. Disappointed after being given that information, we went back across the street, went down in the cellar, and thought about it. It was the general feeling among the group, that although Mister Covington warned against signing the contract, this was an opportunity that we could not pass up. This management company had connections, and they were willing to take a chance on us.

In November 1972 we signed a contract with the WMOT Management Company. I know that Leroy was hurt when we signed with a new management company. We explained to him that WMOT had contacts that he just did not have.

A couple of days later we went to the same apartment where we auditioned with the unsigned contract. When we entered this apartment, it was packed with white people jumping around, dancing, and smoking marijuana. The smell of weed was everywhere. These people were celebrating our signing a contract with the WMOT management company.

When I walked through the apartment, I saw trash bags full of weed. The four of us were led into the kitchen area. We were fed so much marijuana that I was blasted out of my mind. The stems from the marijuana, were heated up between two spoons, while pressing them together. We inhaled the smoke that came off the stems. I considered myself to be an experienced weed smoker but I had never done that before. That just shows how high we were when we signed the contract that day. We did not care. We were young and had never dreamed of having a record deal.

Ted Mills and the Shades of Love joined forces after it was ascertained that the original Blue Magic group was not able to travel. All the original members of Blue Magic were much older and could not handle the choreography necessary to make the group attractive to a younger crowd. This was proven when the group appeared the first time on the Georgie Woods Television Show, a local Philadelphia show. Georgie Woods was a dis jockey on a popular Philadelphia radio Station WDAS. He developed a dance show on television featuring dancing and performances by the best musical groups of the time. This was long before the Soul Train show hit the small screens. His show was the black man's "American Band Stand," featuring Dick Clark. We, (The Shades of Love) tried to help them with their choreography before they appeared on the show, with Ted Mills singing lead on the hit song "Spell." They did a terrible job of following the steps that they had rehearsed. They were so bad that the television cameras could not follow them.

Our management company made the decision to add

Ted to our group as the lead singer. We loved hearing Ted sing on the radio when he was the lead singer of the Toppiks. He was a very private person, who shared very little about himself. I never knew anything about his family background. I never even met his mother. He did have experience in the music business, so on some levels that was a help to us as we became closer as a group, We were satisfied with that arrangement. His ability as a song writer was amazing. He wrote the songs "What's Come Over Me," and" Chasing Rainbows," among other songs that made our group famous. He sang lead on all of those hit songs, thus the new Blue Magic was born.

Ted and I worked well together. However at times he did things that were unexplainable. In some ways I found him to be a strange person. One time he invited me to go to West Philadelphia and hang out with him. When we arrived at our destination, we met up with some guys he knew. Out of the blue he told me that he decided to go with these guys, and that he would see me later. He did not ask me if I knew how to get home or if leaving me was alright? He just abandoned me in a part of the city where I was lost. I was from North Philadelphia and knew nothing about West Philly. I knew nothing about the neighborhood. I knew nothing about the transportation system. He did not even ask me if I had enough money to get home. You do not do that to someone that you consider a friend. I trusted him. That incident told me what type of person he was. I do not think that he thought about what he was doing to me. He put me in panic mode. I looked around and did not know what to do. Then I saw the above ground train station called the "L." I found my way home on public transportation only with the help of people on the street. Thank goodness I did not run into any gangs. Despite experiences like that musically we were on the same page.

I believe that Ted was musical genius. The songs that he wrote were out of this world. He called himself "The Wizard." I believe that he thought outside the box. Because of his exceptional talent he sometimes took things in his life to extremes. He called himself Ted" Wizard" Mills sometimes when he introduced himself. Sometimes he annoyed members of our band. Since he was a music major in college, and who played the piano, he would occasionally suggest some chords that he thought the band could use. Some of the guys told me that they did not like his interference.

Ted loved cats. We used to rehearse at my mother's house in the basement. One time he asked my mother to take care of one of his cats while we were on a road trip. She told him yes, but when he brought the feline over, I think my mother wanted to change her mind. This cat was huge. It was not an ordinary house cat. It was in a large cage and when it looked at me its eyes seem to be saying "I want to eat you!" I found out later that it might have been an Ocelot which was a small cat native to southwestern United States and Mexico. It my understanding that the possession of that type of cat as a domesticated animal was eventually outlawed. My mother was so afraid of that cat that she never let it out of the cage while we were on that road trip.

A rule of the road was that you never bring a pet along. We especially held to that rule because we travelled many places in a car. There was the driver, and the five of us, three in the front, three in the back. Ted decided one road trip to bring his cat Miss Bacon. We got as far as Virginia when the rest of the group decided the cat was too much for us in the car. Although the trunk was full of luggage, Ted put the cat in there. It was summer in the south. The temperature was at least 90 degrees. The poor cat started screaming from the trunk after we had been driving for a while. When we stopped the car and Ted opened the trunk, the cat leaped out and ran off into the woods. Ted chased behind her yelling Miss Bacon, Miss Bacon! A half hour later he had not found the cat, so we told him we had to go. He just loved cats.

Another Ted story involved our performance at the Spectrum in Philadelphia. Our manager was informed by some of the staff that the police were there to take Ted into custody for failure to pay child support. He came into our dressing room and told us what to do. At the end of our performance, we jumped from the stage, ran out into the audience up the isles and got away. Ted was the only member of our group at that time with children. I did not know anything about child support.

Once our group was given the name, and was now gaining some notoriety, I decided to break down for myself what I believe was the definition of Blue Magic. I believed that the spiritual aura which is a part of the body is blue. Most of the colors that we see represent some type of emotion or feeling. The word Magic comes from the word Magi. Magi were the three wise men who came to visit Baby Jesus. I defined Blue Magic to mean the spiritual wise men from the east. I felt that our group was developing a spiritual unit. Suddenly I knew why the group was here. The music we made healed people. It made people fall in love. Our music suggested positive thinking in the minds of those who listened. Our music was called "Soul Music!!" Soul music meant something. It is quite awesome when you think about the fact that we might have thirty musicians playing on one song. There might be fifteen horn players, sixteen people on strings, plus a rhythm section. That was more than thirty individual souls creating MAGIC which was recorded live. That is why I believe that Soul Music will never die. The Soul never dies. We gave life and love through music. I believed us to be musical doctors when we performed. When we hit the stage, we healed the audience by helping them to forget all the stress in their lives. When they listened to our music they forgot about their jobs, paying the bills, and all outside negative distractions. That is what we still do to the people who come to our shows today. We take them back to their teenage and young adult years. We still make audiences forget the problems of the day and remember the great times in the past.

The managers of our record company did not have a lot of money. What they did have was the gift of gab and persuasion. Around this time in Philadelphia there was Kenny Gamble and Leon Huff, who were influential in creating "Philadelphia International Records." They were hot on the Rhythm & Blue music scene. writing and producing songs for Teddy Pendergrass and the O Jay's. Our management company however, was able to take these five young black men into the studio used by Gamble and Huff "Sigma Sound" to record. During our studio time we were able to use the great guitarist and producer Norman Harris. Norman was such a great guy. He gave us the freedom to express ourselves. We were young and did not know anything about the business of recording. Norman must have seen our potential. We did know how to sing. Norman took us to his house, pulled out a box of cassettes, and told us to choose some songs that we liked. The first song that I remember that I liked was "Stop to Start," which we sung on our first album. There were also songs that Ted Mills wrote such as "What's Come Over Me", which was also featured on our first album. Norman was still working with Gamble and Huff, but he was allowed to lend his musical knowledge and talent to our album.

We were also introduced to Linda Creed, who was Tom Bell's musical writing partner. She had been working with the singing groups the Spinners and the Stylistics. Her connection to us was that she knew our managers. Linda was a sweet person. She invited us to her home, that she shared with her husband "Eppy" Epstein. Everyone in the group went to her home except Ted. When we met Eppy he was the manager of the popular band War. Linda was gracious enough to give us some vocal training lessons. That one lesson was not enough. I admit we needed more. None of us had ever had any formal vocal training. During that one session she led us over to her piano and had each one of us sing alone. She never said anything to us after each of us sang. She later told our manager who she thought should sing tenor, baritone, or bass, in ways that would make our harmonies tight. This was a help in deciding who should sing which part on a song. Linda could not work with us on any recordings because she worked for the Philadelphia International Recording Company. It was such a tragedy that she died so young from cancer.

When we started performing, we did not expect that the shows would come one right after the other. Our fans really wanted to hear us. As a result of night after night singing and not knowing how to preserve our voices, we all at some point got strep throat. In my case I thought that smoking cigarettes played a part in losing some of my voice. To this day cigarettes are still the one vice I cannot kick.

The first show we did as Blue Magic was in a small club in Philadelphia call "OOPS." We knew nothing about the financial side of the business. We did know that we were suppose to get paid. It took time for me to figure out that performing was only 10% of the business. The business end was 90%. We received one dollar and seventy- five cent each for that first job as professional singers. It was barely enough money to pay our carfare back to our homes.

Our first major show under our new contract while still using the name The Shades of Love, was to perform as the opening act for the band War in Camden New Jersey. War was hugely popular at this time as a musical band. There manager was able to convince the promoters to put us on the show. We received a great reception from the crowd when we performed.

Later we were scheduled to do a show in Baltimore when Rick got sick. Ted decided that he did not want to go without Rick. Our managers did not want to hear that. Vernon, Keith, and myself had to do the show without them. We did not have our lead singer so we ended up singing the top ten hits made popular by Rhythm and Blues artists. We stood on the bar which we used as a stage and sung our hearts out. Once again we were well received by the audience.

I do not think that WMOT management expected our group to last. During the photo shoot of our first album cover we were told to report to Fairmount Park in Philadelphia where we were promised a wardrobe and a vintage car to pose with. The car was there but there were no clothes for us to change in to. The clothes that you see on the album cover were the clothes that we wore to the shoot. Besides the failure to provide clothes the album cover had dark spots in some cases not showing the faces clearly of some of our members. Once our first album, "Blue Magic" was released, in 1974. It sold a million copies and gave us our first gold record. Songs "Spell, ""Start to Stop," and "What's Come Over Me," all made the top twenty on the Billboard charts. The success of the album made our managers start "tripping!" They thought that they could now compete with Philadelphia International Records. The word got back to Gamble and Huff and subsequently they told Norman not to get involved in a second album. Our managers offered Norman so much money that he decided to do the album despite the orders from his bosses. The first day of recording Norman came to the studio with a broken arm. It was the arm that Norman used to play the guitar. When we asked him what happened, he said that he slipped in his swimming pool. It was winter and his pool was outdoors. Norman did work on the album with the help of guitarist Bobby Eli, who played what Norman was unable to play.

WMOT had visions of developing a stable of young artists and creating their own musical dynasty. Besides Blue Magic they signed, the singing groups Impact, and The Sons of Robinson Stone. They also signed singer Major Harris. Bobby Eli had originally been writing songs just for our group. He told me that he wrote the song "Love Won't Let Me Wait" for me but management decided to give the song to Major Harris as a way of making him a well-known singer in their stable. Had I been able to record that hit song It might have sent my career in another direction.

In our own style we planned to remake the song "It's Gonna Take a Miracle" made popular by a Motown group. We came off the road only to find out that WMOT took singer Denise Williams into the studio and recorded the song which became a hit for her. What I did not like was that the management company was taking the money they made off Blue Magic and expanded their company, without us being financially compensated. We had a contract which did not include what I was upset about. They honored the contract we signed up until now, so that was own us.

During this period, I was aware of a criminal organization called the Black Mafia. I did know a car dealer who was part of the group. I was told by singer Billy Paul that they shot up a club in Atlantic City where he was singing, among other acts of violence. I heard that to keep the performers and managers in line, violence or intimidation was sometimes used. I learned early on that the music industry was a ruthless business. Fortunately, our group however was never subjected to any intimidation.

We signed a contract to be the opening act on a tour in Germany with Ike and Tina Turner. Our first night of the tour, after we performed the audience loved us so much that they screamed over and over "BLUE MAGIC, BLUE MAGIC, BLUE MAGIC! "They even continued this chant when Ike and Tina came out on stage. Ike came to us after the show and asked us to shave down our performance from forty-five to forty minutes. We quickly went to rearranging our medley of songs. The next performance garnered the same results. We had to cut our show again by another fifteen minutes. In Dusseldorf Germany we received the same inspirational applause. Our show was eventually cut down to fifteen minutes before he fired us. We had a contract, so no matter what we did or did not do we still got paid. He tried to explain to us that he thought we were a folk band. I thought to myself after telling us that, why would he hire a band or group for his tour that he never heard? We were able to hang out in London for a couple of weeks on Ike's dime, because of the way the travel arrangement had been set up.

While hanging out in London with some of our band members they asked our manager for some of their pay. He shorted them on what they expected to receive so they were angry to say the least. Our group one evening went out to dinner with our manager. When we returned to the hotel where we were staying, we noticed that the lights on our floor were turned off. When our manager went to open the door to his room, he found that someone had spread feces all over his door knob.

To make matters worse our managers went first to a London newspaper, and once back home to the Philadelphia Tribune and told these periodicals what Ike did to us on the tour. We did not know about this action until we saw the articles in print. I was angry with our managers for making that decision without informing us first. This was one of the times our managers failed to includes us in decisions that could affect our careers.

Ike found out about the articles, and he was pissed. There was a period, when I wondered why our second album, "Magic of the Blue" did not do as well as our first gold record. This album featured such great songs as "Three Ring Circus" written by Bobbi Eli and Vinnie Barrette. I found out that Ike used his tremendous power to threaten the mom-and-Pop small independent radio stations around the country not to play our songs. Ike had a great deal of power in the record industry. He had our songs black balled from being played. This was the consequence of our managers talking to the press about how we were treated on the tour with him. Ike told someone during an interview that he had Blue Magic black balled. I did not realize what happened until during an interview the interviewer made a comment about Blue Magic being Black Balled.

It was a well-known practice at that time that Radio Disk Jockeys could make or break a musical artist's career simply by playing or refusing to play their songs. The way to get your songs played was to give the Disk Jockey a "Brown

Paper Bag" of money under the table. This business practice was known as payola. Disk Jockeys could literally make you a millionaire, by playing your songs in their rotation on the radio. That was the politics of the business. Someone like the popular seventy and eighties Disk Jockey the late Frankie Crocker could make you rich if he played your songs regularly. We met with Frankie in his radio studio and asked him to promote our record "Spell." He responded to our request by telling us that we had to give him a "black bag" meaning payola. I understood the game so we did what was requested. Our song got played. I understood that Disk Jockeys did not make a great deal of money. What else did they get out of the deal? That practice was eventually stopped as the Internal Revenue zeroed in on the unreported income.

Among the any things that I did not know at the time we signed with WMOT was that Randy Cane had a part ownership in the company. Randy was a member of the Delphonics singing group at the time. The managers bought out Randy and offered the popular Philadelphia Disk Jockey Butter Ball, Randy's share of the partnership. That was smart. They now had a Disk Jockey who had a part ownership in the company, who would play their songs on the radio. He then would also get a percentage from the record sales of artists produced by WMOT. Ted Mills also had money invested in WMOT, which he did not initially tell the group about. He was not doing well financially, so WMOT also bought him out.

The new and improved Blue Magic Group performed on the Georgie Woods Television Show, and did well. I ran

Into Mr. Woods one night while we were in a local club. He told me that he did not like my singing group. The reason for his dislike, according to him, was that our group had not paid any dues. What he meant by that was that many of the singing groups that came before us, such as the O Jay's, The Temptations, or The Four Tops, travelled around the country and on tours through what was called the Chitlin Circuit. None of their fame was instant. Many of those famous groups faced segregated theaters and the sting and humiliation and racism. This happened in many of the places they performed, especially in the south. We sold a million albums on our first time out of the gate. Our experiences were different. It was a different time. Groups like the Stylistics and the Futures also achieved instant success. I am grateful for those singing groups who came before us for helping to make our instant success possible.

We also performed on the Jerry Blavat Show, and Dick Clark's American Band Stand television show. Jerry Blavat like Georgie Woods was a local radio disk jockey, in Philadelphia, who parlayed his success into a television dance show featuring the popular singing groups and singer at the at time. Both Jerry and Dick were very cool men who treated us with admiration, respect, and encouragement. During our Unsung session on television's BET network, we were seen performing on the beach during one of our times on American Bandstand.

Among the groups and singers that we performed with over the years were The Temptations, Glady Knight, and the Pips. The Jackson Five, The Manhattans, the Stylistics,

Billy Paul, Luther Vandross, Ray, Goodman, and Brown, and Harold Melvin and the Blue notes. Some of the other talented performed were The Soul Generation, War, Issac Hayes, Ike and Tina Turner and comedians Richard Pryor and Eddie Murphy.

Chapter 5
"It's Like Magic"

With the success of our first album that went gold the money started flowing. I had so much money or at least what I thought was serious money, that I did not know what to do with it all. I threw a thousand dollars in the air, and did not think twice about it. No one expected our first album to go gold. It might have gone Platinum but there was no such category as Platinum back then. I do know now that I did not get all the money that I was entitled too. I co-wrote and recorded a song with Ted titled "Looking for a Friend." Our voices sounded so much alike that he sang the first verse and I sang the second verse. No one could tell the difference. I thought that when the song was released, he would put me down as one of the writers. He did not, so I was not entitled to any Royalties. I knew nothing about publishing or writer's credits. Ted used to call me and ask me to come over to his house to help him write a song. He never gave me any credit for my help. This is something else that cost me money because I did not understand this side of the business.

An example of someone who understood the business was a man by the name of Al Felder. He understood how the business worked and how to get paid. Norman might be writing a song and something in the lyrics did not fit. Al might give him just one word which made the song work. Al got a writer's credit for just adding one or two words. He was able to get his name listed as a writer on many songs that way.

Once Blue Magic received a gold record, writers were throwing songs our way. They knew that if we sung one of their songs on any of our next albums that meant a pay check.

We signed our Power of Attorney over to management, so checks and our other affairs could be taken care of while we were traveling. That was one of our early mistakes. There were no cellphones, pagers, or fax machines around during this period of time. Giving someone your Power of Attorney was powerful. Management might receive a check in our name. They were able to not only deposit the check but could also withdraw money from my account without permission. Not understanding anything about bookkeeping made it easy to be ripped off. I am not saying that we were cheated because I had no proof, it was just a feeling that I had after learning more how business was conducted. My lack of understanding in this area added to the problem. Business is not conducted like that anymore. There are fax machines, computers, and many other electronic devices which can be used to conduct business now between the artist and their business managers.

Once I started making money no one told me anything about investing or saving some of my money. We were told nothing about getting financial advisers, or even investing in a business. The philosophy in our business was not to tell anyone anything they did not know. The less you knew made it easy for someone to take advantage of you. Ted had some experience in the business before joining Blue Magic, and even he did not suggest anything that could help my financial future. We became successful overnight. It was more than I ever dreamed of. It felt good to have money in my pocket and adoring fans, especially the women. I was not thinking long term about life. I was not thinking about what was going on in the office. I just wanted to enjoy the moment.

We were not the only group that might have been taken advantage of financially. Some of the top black singing groups during this period were also having similar problems. We were making more money that we could ever dreamed of on the road, so we were satisfied with what we were getting. We all were young with no real responsibilities. We later found out that the road money was only a portion of the profits we were owed. We never thought about what was happening back home. We did not know how the system worked. In hindsight we should have hired a personal attorney who would have looked out for our interest. It was only later through our experiences did we figure out what we should do. Ignorance is bliss except when it comes to business.

When a show is booked a deposit, usually half the total contract is sent to our management company. They then would take their money from the deposit. There then was no need to go on the road with the group because they had already been paid. It was the road managers responsibility to collect the remaining money from the contract and pay our group. The first time we found out how we were being cheated we were performing in California with Ray, Goodman, and Brown. Our booking agent sent a representative out to collect our money. Since we did not see the need for him to come out to California because the booking agency had already received their money in the deposit for the show, we questioned what was going on? When we did not get a satisfactory explanation from the agency representative, we spoke with the promoter, who told us that he paid far more money than we were led to believe for our performances. I did look at the contract and was satisfied. What I found was there were two contracts. One we were shown, and the second was given to the management company. We might have been shown a contract telling us that we would be paid five thousand for the show, when management received seven thousand.

Years later I was told by people in the industry that we were laughed at. They said that we were not being treated fairly, and everyone knew it; everyone but us. Kenny Gamble of the great writing team Gamble and Huff sometimes would come watch us rehearse. He knew what was going on with our management but stayed out of their business arrangements with our group. I wish that we could have collaborated with them. They along with Tom Bell and Linda Creed were putting out some beautiful music. Once again on paper WMOT did honor their contract, however we failed to read the words behind the words.

One time we only received a Royalties check of sixty thousand dollars to be split among five people. That was a joke. We thought you worked, you got paid. We never thought about Royalties. In the mean while our managers were doing the right things, buying properties, apartment buildings, and investing the profits from the sale of our records and promoting other groups or singer. I believe that the place where we lost the most money was on our overseas trips. On those trips we were accompanied by someone from management, who always collected our money and then would pay the group members.

There were a few occasions when we were told by the promoters that they did not have all the money before we performed, but that we would be given a check for the balance.. When we went to cash the checks later, they bounced. At that point there was very little we could do.

There was a show that we did for singer Johnny Taylor in a club. He promised to pay us after the show once he got all the receipts from the door and the bar. We went to his room after the show, where Ted asked him for our money. Johnny put a gun on the table in front of him while his three henchmen, looked on. He then said "Look Pete I don't have your money!" The gun suggested that if we were going to start trouble we could be shot. All we could do was to just leave the room unpaid. On the job training was how we learned how not to get ripped off. Later after understanding how the game was played Vernon and I set up our own company. It was named the Sawyer Brothers Publishing company.

Another person who did it to us was Cuba Gooding Senior, the father of the actor Cuba Gooding Junior. He booked us to do a show with him in New Jersey. After the show Cuba told us that he had to go to the bank and withdraw our money. He had been an accomplished star from sometime so we trusted him. We had plans to go to a club in New York City so he told us he would meet us there. He never showed. He went to his grave owing money to Blue Magic.

We had the same problem in Newark, New Jersey before another show. Because our past experiences we did not take any promoter at his word. We had been burned enough times to not allow it to happen anymore. I was chosen by the group to go out on stage and tell the audience that we were not going to perform because we had not been paid. The promoter was angry. Too bad, but we did what we had to do, because our fans would have blamed us for not performing. It was important to us for everyone see that it was the promoter's fault.

In Jamaica West Indies we were scheduled to do a show. This show featured Blue Magic, Ray, Goodman, and Brown and The Barkay's. We were in the hotel waiting for the promoter to give us our money, when we found out that he flew off the Island with the proceeds from the show. People were waiting for the show to begin. We refused to perform without being paid. The Jamaican authorities sent the army to our hotel with automatic weapons and covered every exit. Since the promoter flew us in to Jamaica, we figured everything was cool. We had round trip tickets. A Jamaican representative told us that no one was leaving from the island until a show was performed, or people got their money back. Ray, Goodman, and Brown decided to go and perform as they felt it was not the people's fault that the promoter was a crook. We did have a two day vacation on the island, as a result of this incident. Since we did not perform and had round trip tickets, we did not try to find the promoter who set up the concert.

I was not only unhappy with how we were being treated by our management, after learning more about how the business was conducted. I wanted more control over our future. I also felt that we were disrespected. We were told that we were going to receive the Ebony Award. We were not given any information as to when the televised event was to take place. Management failed to inform us. We were then sent on the road. The day of the awards ceremony we received a call from management. They informed us that the ceremony was that night, and since were not able to attend a representative would go up on stage and get the award for us. We would have loved to attend such an honorable event. I watched the show in my hotel room. Until this day I never saw the award. I will admit that if not for WMOT we would never have been stars.

Many young artists today are still not educated as to how to navigate the business end of the music business. We tried educating New Edition backstage before one of their performances. We saw them as our little brothers. We unsuccessfully tried to get into their dressing room. Our purpose was to school them on why they should watch their money. There was no proof that anything of a fiduciary nature was going wrong. We just wanted to make sure they understood what was going on as a courtesy. I just wanted them to learn from my mistakes. We saw at that time that they were being managed by two white guys so we just wanted to make sure that what was happening to us was not happening to them. Their security would not let us meet with them in their dressing room backstage.

Early in our career WMOT bought a raggedy van for our group to use from singer Barbara Mason. One of our managers drove the vehicle down to Washington DC where we were performing. The next day we had a show in Boston and were expected to drive the van there. The first problem with the van was that there were no back seats so anyone who was not driving or sitting in the shotgun seat had to sit on the metal floor in the back. Travelling with me in the small truck were Ted, Rick, Keith and Ron Woodson, our driver who we called Rabbit. Vernon did not make the trip with us because he had to return to Philadelphia to take care of some legal matters. I did not understand why they bought a vehicle that at best needed a lot of work. To make our problem even worse was that the van could not go any faster than twenty miles an hour. You could push the accelerator pedal to the floor and still only twenty miles an hour. I thought that the clutch was going causing this problem. Our final problem was that because it was a clutch driven vehicle no one other than Rabbit knew how to drive it. Ted had a driver's license so he would give Rabbit a break by driving. When he had a problem shifting gears, he would wake Rabbit up for assistance. We did manage to drive all the way to Boston under those conditions. and made our performance on time. Management never repaired the van. They just got rid of it. That was the only vehicle that was purchased for the group. All transportation after that was owned by our road managers.

We had many road managers over the years. George Franklin was our first. We found out early in our relationship with him that he was reporting back to WMOT everything that we did on the road. We saw him as a spy. At that point we knew that he could not be trusted. One night as George was dropping Ted off at his apartment, they got into a heated argument about George's telling WMOT everything he saw us do on the road. As Ted exited the car, he told George that he was nothing but a "Brown noser." He further told him that his head was stuck up management's ass! I was sitting in the front seat next to George when he reached across me and in the glove compartment, where he pulled out a gun. He then exited the car, where the two continued to argue at the rear of the vehicle. Suddenly, I heard two loud gun shots POW POW! I looked back and realized that George had fired two shots into the ground out of anger. Ted did not flinch. He just walked away. Looking back at George, he said "I will see you later!" When George got back in the car I was scared as shit because I knew he was angry and he had a gun. Since I already did not trust him, I hoped he would not take out his anger on me.

Another time we had a show in Washington DC. Our agreement with WMOT was always if we stayed in a hotel, that cost was deducted for what we made on the show. Keith and I found a couple of ladies that we could stay with for the week we were there. We planned to get that money since we had no hotel bill. When the trip ended George refused to pay us the money that we were owed. Making things worse he told us that we owed him money.

A week later we were in Atlanta Georgia to do a show. Keith and I were roommates. We decided that now was a good time to talk to George about the money we were owed. I suggested to Keith that we should do this in a diplomatic way. When we walked to George's room, to my surprise Keith immediately without knocking, kicked the door in and pulled out a gun. I was shocked, because I did not know that Keith had a gun. George ran across his room and grabbed his gun. Watching this I took off running. I did not want to get caught in the middle of a gunfight. I looked back as I ran and saw that Keith was right on my heels. We got back to our room, which was only two or three doors from George's room safely. The rest of the day Keith and George were constantly popping their heads in and out of their rooms looking for each other. The next day we noticed that our limousine was gone. George detached the trailer which carried the bands instruments and our clothes from the car. He left us stranded in Atlanta. Our band had their own travel band, so they were alright. We explained to the promoter of the show what happened. She was gracious enough to pay our ways back to Philadelphia. Once home we told WMOT management what happened. They yelled at George but did not fire him. I do not think that George cared what they thought. He sat there during the lecture and just said "Yeah, Yeah, Yeah," while almost ignoring them. I was pretty sure that George was also stealing money from us.

The first car we used on the road was not owned by WMOT. It was a black Cadillac. The Caddy was owned by George our road manager. The car for some unexplained reason had scratches and dents that ran the full length of the right side. It looked like the vehicle had been side swiped. When we pulled up to a theatre, where we were performing, we always parked in a way that you only saw the side of the car that was not damaged. We were supposed to be a" Big Time" singing group, yet we were riding around in a dented car. It was embarrassing.

Pop Montague was our second road manager. He was tricky too. He was once the road manager for Patti Labelle. On the road Pop always carried a bag. He did not allow anyone to touch that bag. I happened to pick it up one time and realized how heavy it was. I knew that he did not have clothes in the bag because he wore the same apparel all the time. He would yell at anyone who touched this bag. Every time we performed in the Washington DC area, he would get together with a dark skin woman, and they would always go back to his room in the hotel. We did a lot of flying during this time. Pop always tipped the sky caps that carried our bags. On one trip we got hold of the receipts concerning the tips. Something was wrong. We knew that Pop had not spent that much money in tips. We noticed that every time we entered that airport terminal Pop would summon the assistance of the same sky cap. That was when one of the airport guys told us what Pop was doing. In that heavy bag he was carrying a machine that could be used to print out receipts. He was using that machine to make receipts with higher costs spent than what he really spent. The mysterious dark skin woman who always visited his room was good at helping him make the right calculation on each receipt. These were the types of things that people did to rip us off.

Then there was "Hot Dog." He was "Super Fly" in the way he dressed. We met him when we performed in St Louis. During one of our conversations, I gave him my address in Philadelphia. Soon after we met, he began lobbying us to become our road manager. Hot Dog was a St Louis pimp. He even had the pimp car with the fur lined steering wheel and dash board. Since Hot Dog wanted to become our road manager this caused friction between him and our current manager. Nario Wright was our road manager, at that time. We were sitting in our hotel room one night after a show when Nario and Hot Dog started arguing. At some point during the argument Nario said to Hot Dog "You must be on your Period!" Hot Dog was from the street. He was not going to be emasculated. He leaped across the bed on Nario and they started fighting. We had to pull them apart. I cannot say who won the fight, before we pulled them apart. Nario was really a nice guy, and a good road manager. I trusted him. He passed away sometime within the past several years, of this publication..

Two weeks after we performed in St Louis Hot Dog showed up at my mother's house in Philadelphia. He had nowhere to live. He thought he could stay with us in my mother's place. I told him no way. My guess is that he used his skill as a pimp to find housing. Eventually Hot Dog did become the Master of Ceremony of our shows.

The next Master of Ceremony we had called himself "Fashion Plate." He was put in charge of our wardrobes along with other duties. At some point during our relationship, he started having money problems. I was never sure if it was our fault or that of WMOT. Backstage before one of our shows when we went to put on our costumes, we noticed that they smelled like piss. We found out that Fashion Plate had urinated on our clothes, because he was mad with us over his money. We poured cologne all over ourselves to disguise the odor the best we could. We had to let him go after what he did. People would do some strange things over money.

There were also occasional disputes over money with some of the band members. One memorable dispute took place when travelling to New Jersey in our touring car when a tire blew out. When we went to get the tire repaired, we were told that someone had slashed the tire. The mechanic told us that he thought someone wanted us to die.

As the Shades of Love, we went to many shows and studied how the different groups performed and the reception they got from the audiences. Thinking about it now watching those groups were motivating forces for us all, as well as being educational. While sitting in a theatre watching a group perform, we noticed that they had very little choreography. It was not even close to what we put together. What I did see was that they had the attention of the crowd. If you can get the attention of your audience, suggested that you are getting other people to recognize what you are doing. That is worth more than money. Naturally when I started my music careers, I wanted to get paid, but I was not in the business just for the money. I got such pleasure from seeing the looks on the faces of our fans. It was hard to describe the feelings. I think that is part of the problem with some artists today. They think about the money first. We did not care whether there were two people or twenty thousand people in the audience we put on the best show possible. Our virtuosity as singers dictated that we always do the best. I have seen artists not want to do their best because of the size of the crowd. That attitude always bothered me.

Keith was our choreographer. He did a great job of helping us move across the stage and tell a story behind the lyrics to each song. We all participated in helping to arrange the steps, but Keith was the main man. He was the best. His orchestrations were so admired that we were told by Brooke Pain the person who created the singing group New Edition, that he modeled their movements after ours. Brooke said that after seeing our show in Boston he went out in search of five young men who could sing and move on stage like we did. I believe we had the best choreography going at the time of our popular hits. We out did most groups when it came to moves on stage.

Ted had two left feet, he could not dance, but it did not matter because he was the lead singer. It was funny sometimes watching him try to keep up with us. Rick was not that great of a dancer either, but he did the best he could. We fed off each other and made it work like "Magic." Many times, our dance moves matched the horn section that played behind us. We always had to be in rhythm with the horns for everything to work.

There was a point in our careers, when we were told that the famous Motown choreographer Charlie {Cholly} Atkins was going to show us some of his moves. While California we met with Cholly, who wanted us to do some steps that he put together for our upcoming show.

The song we performed the steps to was "Magic of the Blue." While performing on stage to the song for the first time, I looked around and saw Keith and Ted run into each other, landing on the floor. It did not take long for us to realize that what Charlie Atkins wanted us to do did not fit our style.

We performed at Radio City Music Hall in New York,with The Jackson Five. We went out on stage first and brought the house down. The audience loved us. The next day there was an Amsterdam Newspaper article stating that "Blue Magic took the show from the Jackson Five." I realized later why we were more appealing to the crowd at that show. The Jackson Five had just come from doing a Vegas show. They came out on stage with chairs and props that might have been popular in Vegas, but not New York. They should have just been The Jackson Five that made all of those hit records. Every time we performed in California after that show, I would notice four limousines always pulling up during our sound checks. Out of those limousines came Jackie, Marlon, Jermaine, and Tito. They would stand back stage and just look at us. While backstage they always greeted us, but never explained why they were there. Years later I thought about their visits. I believe that their father, Joe Jackson, probably told them to go study, our routines. He remembered what we did in New York. Later in life I tried to find the article from the Amsterdam News that was published about that show. I could not find it anywhere.

While in New York someone set up a celebrity basketball game in Harlem. The Jackson Five and Blue Magic against a local basketball team. I played basketball, and I was pretty good; but I was not crazy about it. I made a mistake during the game, and Jackie Jackson started yelling at me. I responded to his tirade by telling him that I was just trying to have fun. I told him that he needed to be cool. The local team we played against were semi- professional; we were singers, I reminded him. The team we played against had matching uniforms. and were like a machine on the court. We came out in shorts and sneakers. They kicked our asses. I later found out that Jackie was serious about his basketball. He always wanted to win which explained his attitude during that promotional game.

We used to do cover songs, which were songs previously performed by other artists. The song "I'll Be Around" by the Spinners I performed. Vernon sung, "I Don't Want to Be Lonely" written by Bobby Eli. This song was recorded by the Main Ingredients featuring Cuba Gooding on one of their albums. We were also able to record the song on our first album, with Bobby Eli playing guitar. He was the guitarist with Mother, Father, Sister, Brother orchestra known as MFSB. This was the band that played behind the hits of the O Jay's, Teddy Pendergrass, and most of the hot groups in the Philadelphia International stable at that time.

We decided to open our shows with these cover songs because it gave Ted a chance to warm up. This worked well until after completing three albums. Our band Conductor Bryan Williams finally told us that we needed to stop with the cover songs because the people came to hear us sing the songs made popular on our albums. We took his advice.

CHAPTER 6
"LET THERE BE LOVE"

Rick was the first member of our group to get married. He married his childhood sweetheart at eighteen before we formed our group. She slowly became less supportive of his being on the road. I always thought that, she screwed his brains out before every road trip, because he never messed around with any girls. I guess it could have been because he felt guilty about leaving her at home and he loved her. Women found him attractive but he would not bite. I remember this one time a white woman followed us all over Texas trying to get Rick's attention. We would pull into a town and she would be there already yelling "I'm here!" He just was not into women the way the rest of us were.

I was the second member of the group to marry. I was twenty-one years old. I had money now because of our successful albums. I met my wife through her cousin who was dating my brother Vernon. She told me that she had a cousin that she wanted me to meet. We were living at 844 N 16th Street in North Philadelphia. She came to visit our house with her cousin. That was where we first met. I thought she was cute. She was just a little thing. I was seventeen years old she was fourteen. I never thought to ask her how old she was because her cousin was my age. We started hanging out together. I would sneak down to see her at her grandmother's house, where she spent a great deal of time. That was where we first had sex. She was a virgin. We had been kissing and fondling each other for a while when I decided I had to have some of that. Her grandmother lived on the first floor of a three-story house. There was a vestibule just before you entered the house. That was where we had sex for the first time. She did not want to, but I was ready.

She lived with her mother and stepfather in an area around Broad Street and Lehigh Avenue. I would take the subway to visit her. We were supposed to be going together, but then I began hearing about another guy who lived in her grandmother's neighborhood, who she might have also been seeing. One evening I was talking to her on the phone and she sounded kind of funny. I got the impression from her lack of conversation that she did not want to talk. Sensing something was wrong I asked Keith to accompany me to her house. There were gangs in her neighborhood so I needed backup if we had to fight our way out of there. I knocked on the front door and did not get an answer. I knew she was home, so I knocked again this time harder. She answered the door this time fearing that the knock might wake up her parents. I asked her what was going on? She answered shyly, "Nothing." The lights were off in the downstairs area, which made me think that something just was not right. I immediately walked back into the kitchen where I saw the pretty boy that I had been hearing about sitting at the kitchen table. I was shocked and hurt, at the same time. I just walked out of the house without saying anything.

We did continue our romance even after that incident. Our romance resulted in her getting pregnant. I was eighteen at the time and she was fifteen years old. I really did not want nor was I prepared to have a child. I knew nothing about options such as abortions at that time. If I had been aware of that option, I might have encouraged her to have one. I was not even at the hospital when my son was born, because I just did not want a child. I remember walking down the street with her during a snowstorm when she was about seven months pregnant wishing that she would fall and abort the baby. I knew that how I felt was wrong but that was how I felt at that time. I knew I was not ready to be a father. There was one thing that I did know for sure, and that was if I had to be a father, I did not want to be the type of man that my father had been. I was afraid of the responsibility that I would be facing. I felt that at eighteen life was just beginning for me. I felt having this baby meant my life would be over. Wendell Junior was born on May 19 1970. I never forgot seeing her and pretty boy together, so when my son came into the world, I looked for evidence that he might not be mine. My obsession was such that I noticed a small light mark on his face and I wondered where it came from. The pretty boy I had seen her with was a light complexion. I talked with the doctor who told me what to get from the pharmacy to make the mark disappear. It worked. This just goes to show how I questioned her at the time. Gradually I began to realize that my son did not choose to be born so I had to be more responsive to his needs. The problem then became that I was starting to travel with Blue Magic so I was never home. My son's mother continued to live at home and take care of him.

Three years later, I married her and she moved into my apartment. I was making good money, so I wanted her to move in with me. Her mother was against us living together so we got married. It was a small wedding ceremony with just our families and close friends. I tried to be a good father to my son, but always travelling he did not see me that much. I was working forty weeks out of the year. I left him and his mother when he was seven years old. I was using a lot of drugs at the time, so that became more important.

Later in life I looked back and I had many regrets concerning how I treated my son and my family. Junior and I did get together after he became a young man. We talked constantly over the phone since I lived in New York and he still lived in Philadelphia. He told me that he forgave me for my behavior while he was growing up. Telling me that made him more of a man than I had ever been. We had good conversations about God. We had excellent discussions about what it meant to be a man with responsibilities. He drove up to New York on an occasion, sought me out, and shared things about his life. I was proud to hear that he had his own car, his own house and, a son of his own. Some of these things I had not accomplished. He learned from my mistakes telling me that he would always be there for his son. Sadly he passed away at the age of forty from a brain tumor.

Watching him wither away and then die was one of the most difficult things that I ever had to deal with in my life. It was such a helpless feeling to be in the hospital and have his doctors tell me that even after his surgery there was nothing else that they could do for him. I miss him and think about him all the time.

I do not believe that any man should get married at

the young age of twenty-one. We are just beginning to experience adult life, and very few men that age are mature enough to handle what is expected in a marriage. It was even more of a bad decision for me when you consider that I was a part of a popular singing group. I was expected to be faithful. I never thought about that until I got on the road with Blue Magic and was married. I was not faithful to my wife. I left her stuck at home dealing with child care, while I was on the road. My behavior was just wrong. There is no excuse that I can give to justify what I did.

Whenever I performed in New York there was this one woman who would always come to my hotel room. She always gave me a blowjob during our encounters. This one time I wanted to have sex, which we did. Nine months later she started spreading the word that she had my son. She named the boy Wendell. When my wife found out about this child, she went ballistic in my hotel room. She began to throw things everywhere, while telling me that she hated me. I denied having another child or even knowing about another child, which was true. I never knew how my wife found out about the baby that was supposed to be mine. She confronted me about the situation, before I even knew about it myself. I do know that women talk. I thought she might have heard about it from another woman. I know I did not tell her or anyone else, because I did not know myself.

My daughter Shemeka was born on November 24 1977. When she was born, I had questions once again. She was a very light complexion when born. Since my aunt Mamie was a light complexioned woman while my mother and her other sister aunt Lillie were of a darker hue my suspicions about color were less than when my son was born. I however knew that the pretty boy was never totally out of the picture, so that thought continued to haunt me. Someone told me that they were seen going into a bar together while I was on the road. People I knew from my neighborhood planted doubts in my head with comments such as, "So you think that she is your daughter?" I even wondered if her decision to have another baby was payback, possibly with another man because I was alleged to have impregnated another woman. There was no proof that I was the father of that baby. I think that she wanted to believe it was true. She was not stupid she knew of my past infidelity. In the end all that did not matter. I accepted Shemeka as my daughter. I had no intentions of getting any DNA tests. I did have doubts for a long time, but that was my guilt and insecurity. I got over it. Shemeka is my daughter.

Years later I was talking to a member of the Delphonics singing group who mentioned to me that he had been working with my son Wendell. I thought he was talking about my son Wendell Junior. I told him that I did not know that my son was involved with music. Talking further, he explained to me that he was talking about my son who lived in the Poconos. I realized then who he was talking about. This Wendell was the son of my former sex partner. I got his phone number and called him. During our conversation he told me that his mother always said that I was his father. I thought to myself during our conversation "wow I only slept with his mother one time."

There was someone that I met in Bach elementary school who became one of my friends. What made

Bach Elementary unique was that it was in an all-white neighborhood, but there were only a few white children in my school. Many of the white kids in the neighborhood either went to Catholic or private schools. There were no elementary schools in my black neighborhood. One day my friend broke a glass by accident in a store near our school. The police were called. They started hassling this poor kid, when my mother who happened to be in the store with me at the time, yelled at the police to leave the child alone." He did not do anything wrong." she said. To my surprise the police let him go. We introduced ourselves. That is how we met. That was the beginning of our being friends. Our friendship continued even though we went to different high schools.

Now fast forward, I am now a member of Blue Magic. I just came off the road early and was relaxing in my apartment. My wife was not home. There was a knock on the door. The man who considered my friend was standing there when I opened it. He looked surprised to see me. I quickly asked him why he was standing at my front door, since we had not seen each other in sometime. He nervously responded that he was just in the neighborhood and decided to stop by. I immediately flashed back to what he said to me one time in the past when we were together. He told me that my wife was pretty. Now I suspected he had been popping by my place to visit my wife when I was on the road. It was evident to me that he did not expect me to be home. I felt that if you are going to come by my place, call first to make sure I am off the road. Keith had previously warned me to watch him around my wife. He cautioned me, because he said that he had approached his girlfriend. Keith called him a snake. It was situations like that which made me suspicious of what was happening at home while I was on the road. It was all rumors and my insecurity that made me feel that way. I had proof that anything was happening while I was away

What was interesting was that through most of our marriage my wife and I got along well together. We did not fight at all. We lived in a newly built apartment complex located at Front and Godfrey Streets. There were very few black people living there. No one bothered us, for the most part. There was however one time I was walking down the street when a car load of white boys passed me and yelled nigger several times. A supermarket was being built across the street which made it convenient. Rick also moved into the complex with his wife and two daughters. We were like one big family. My children played with his kids. Brenda picked out all the furniture, except a bar that I wanted. Life was good.

Keith and Vernon were the last two to get married. Ted never did.

Once we all started making money, everybody in the group got their own apartments, everybody except my brother Vernon. He stayed with my mother until he married his wife Elaine and moved to New York. I do not know if he was just trying to save money, but he stayed put.

Vernon met his wife Elaine, who was from New York at one of our shows. She was a fan who frequented our performances. They got married and did not tell anyone.

When Keith decided to "Jump the Broom" I tried to

talk him out of it. He did not hear me because he was in love. My girlfriend at the time, and I went to the wedding in New Jersey. On the way back to New York our car broke down. Vernon his wife Elaine and her sister saw us stranded on the side of the road and just drove by us without as much as to stop and make sure we were alright. Elaine did not like my current girlfriend. I can only surmise that her dislike for her sprang from their first meeting when the four of us rode somewhere together. Vernon and I were in the front seat and the two of them sat in the back. During the ride she began to talk about her success as an entertainer. She was not bragging but she was proud to have been in the movie The Wiz and on a couple of television shows. I can only guess that was the beginning of Elaine's animosity toward her.

We were young men with a bunch of popular hit songs. In the 1970's we had three top twenty albums and seven top twenty singles. Women were everywhere and we were not turning anything down. We had decided that every city we went to, each of us was going to get a woman to spend the night with us. That was our pact. In Durham North Carolina we performed in a barn. We even changed for the show in a room next to farming equipment. The lighting in the barn was dim at best. Vernon and Rick roomed together and Keith and I roomed together. We talked two women into coming back to our hotel room. I was rapping hard to get the women to spend the night. Keith did not do any talking. He left that up to me.

I finally convinced them to come to our hotel room and stay. I turned off the lights and immediately heard Keith getting busy in bed. The girl Keith was with, looked like a cow. She had two big plats in her hair that made her look like she had horns. She was also heavy. The woman I was with was dark skin and had a nice body. She had an average looking face but was not beautiful. We had a night of lustful sex. We were all to meet up the next morning. The two women that spent the night with us were able to drive themselves home, as mine had her own car. We met the rest of the group by our touring car. When we arrived at the location of our touring car we saw the women the rest of the group had coupled with. Ted had a woman that looked like a witch including the pointed nose. Vernon's overnight date looked like Popeye the sailor, and Rich had a woman who looked like some type of ant. She was a little female, dark skin, with a pointed face. He now stopped resisting female advances.

The ladies had no money to get home, so we gave them money for a cab. Ted did not know what we did, so he put them in our car and told us we were going to drive them home. Keith knew that we gave them carfare so he told them to get out of our car. While riding in the car we talked about how ugly the women were that we picked up in Durham. That was the only place on any of our tours where we picked up what we thought were ugly women. No disrespect to Durham North Carolina but those women were not on the right side of pretty. I do not want to be cruel but they all looked like animals.

In Washington DC after one of our shows as we left the building, the women were lined up as usual. I was approached by a nice-looking white woman. She asked me,

"What do you want tonight, white or black?" I had never been with a white girl, so I took her back to my hotel room. I swallowed a tab of acid and then we got into it. We were screwing all over the room. the bed, the chair, and the table. At some point I was screwing her so hard that blood shot out of her vagina and hit the wall. She fell out of the bed onto the floor. I thought at that point that I killed the woman. She was alright. She left the next day and I never saw her again.

We performed in Buffalo New York. To stay true to our pact we had night guests. It was snowing at a blizzard level. The next morning there was a knock on the door. It was Rick's wife and my mine. They had driven all the way to Buffalo in the heavy snow storm. Our road manager George Franklin's room was right next to ours, so we passed the naked women carrying their clothes into his room across a small connected balcony. The floor in our room was wet with snow, but we cleaned it up the best we could before opening the door. It just so happened that our drummer's wife who also drove up to Buffalo with our wives was sitting in their car outside of the hotel and saw us pass the women from room to room. I denied any involvement with any women. To this day, I never admitted anything. Five years later we returned to Buffalo for a show and those same women approached us at our hotel. The only difference was now they were both big and fat so we did not recognize them until they refreshed our memories. Five years made a big difference in how they looked.

Female groupies were everywhere in every city. The flesh was weak. We were young viral young men. Who could blame us? One time we were staying in a motel in New Jersey. Keith had a woman in his room and went to visit a girl in another room in the same motel. He had to figure out how to leave one woman and get to the woman in the other room. Our road manager at the time, Turk volunteered to drive his car next to the room Keith wanted to leave, blocking the view of the other room. Keith used the vehicle to cover him as he went from one room to another. He was successful in pulling it off and there was no drama.

In Japan I dated a woman who was into black men. When we walked down the street, I saw the looks of prejudice on the faces of the Japanese people. Racism was alive and well even in Japan.

An interesting thing happened on that visit to Japan. During one of our shows in the women audience went going wild. I however noticed that there were Japanese men all dressed in black sitting in thirty tables right in front of the stage. These men had women at these tables with them who stood up and clapped after each song. The men in black just sat in their seats showing no emotion. They did stand up and clap at the end of our performance, with the rest of the crowd. I thought that action was weird. I did until I was informed that those men were members of the Japanese mafia. I did not know that there was a Japanese mafia. I also found out that they paid twenty-five hundred per table.

While in Frankfort Germany on one of our trips, our tour guide took us to a multi floor whore house. When I walked through the house, I noticed that some of these beautiful prostitutes closed their doors. I guessed that they did not want to service black men. I decided to visit the room of a woman who had a German Shepard dog as her companion or body guard. I handed her the agreed upon amount for her services. She took the money, looked me up and down and then told me to leave the room. I asked for my money back and she refused. When I approached her after she refused to give me back my money, the dog started to growl at me so I decided that I better leave. No sex and no money. Once outside the building I was told that these prostitutes were told that black men had tails. That was the same story told about black men as far back as World War I. Now I was sure why doors closed as we walked the halls of the house. It was hard to imagine that even whores could be prejudiced, but they were. I also found out sometime later that the woman and her dog were involved in recorded bestiality.

I admit that I had been with so many women around the world that I could not remember them all. We were in New Mexico where we were followed by four women wherever we went. Keith convinced the nicest looking one of them to come back to his room. Later, that evening we commented when we met up with Keith that we knew that he tore her up! He answered by telling us that when she took off her panties across the room, he could smell an offensive odor coming from between her legs. He told her to put her clothes back on and get the hell out of his room. You must believe that if she smelled bad from across the room it must have been very bad.

There was a stripper or Go- Go dancer, which they called themselves at that time, that I liked to see in Philadelphia at a club. Her stage name was "Black Beauty." The name was appropriate. She was gorgeous. She had a perfect body, with beautiful dark chocolate colored skin. One night Keith and I went to the club. When the evening ended we talked Black Beauty and her sister into joining us. We decided to rent a hotel room. I started screwing Black Beauty on one side of the room and Keith went to work on her sister on the other side of the room. I finished and Keith was still going. I went twice before Keith finished once. I realized then how much staying power he had. Three days later I started itching. I found out that this beautiful stripper 'Burnt Me,'" meaning she gave me an STD. What made that incident worse was that I gave that sexually transmitted disease to a woman who lived in Washington D.C. that I really cared about. She had nothing to do with me after I transmitted the disease to her.

Like many entertainers Blue Magic had our own personal physician. Being as sexually active as we were we needed his medicines when we contracted venereal diseases. Thank goodness he was good at what he did. Collectively we had this problem so many times that he gave me a big bottle of tetracycline, which is an antibiotic, with instructions for all of us to take before having sex. If any of the group needed the pills I had them in my room, when we travelled.

A funny story concerning the doctor happened. He had to give each of us a series of seven vaccinations before we went to London. When it was Keith's turn the doctor stuck the needle in his butt and he immediately screamed and started running around the room with the needle flopping around in his ass. I was in shock because I had never seen anything like that. The doctor on the other hand just laughed at the situation.

There came a time when I got tired of the lying, and cheating on my wife, I always knew that it was wrong but I did it anyway. I wanted to eradicate drug use, and all the negative activities associated with being on the road in the music business. It was at that point that I decided to start the study of religion. On one of our tours, we went to the country of Malaysia. We were treated like royalty everywhere that we went. The night life was out of this world. Every night my fellow group members would hit the clubs. Not me. There was nothing wrong with what they were doing. That is what entertainers do, including me. My thought process now was pointing me in a different direction. I decided that I was going to take this opportunity to study the Bible. I set a goal of reading the complete book. My interpretation of what I read in that book was trying to tell me." Too much of anything is no good for you." That interpretation described how I was feeling about the night life. Something was now beginning to push me in another direction. I knew that I was tired of the way I was living.

The longest relationship I had with any woman was 15 years. The second longest relationship was 11 years. I have counted what I would call four major relationships in my life. When I cut the ties, it was not always their faults. I have always been turned on by attractive women who were crazy as hell. All accept my wife. I did a lot of dirt in my life, and I am still haunted by my past behavior.

CHAPTER 7
"ALL L REALLY NEED IS YOU"

Blue Magic was a family. In our best times, if you messed with one of us you had to deal with the other four. We performed a show in New York, where I met a woman after the show. I took her back to my room, for a night of lust. The next night I heard all this commotion backstage, while I was getting ready for the show. Keith came running into the dressing room, to warn me that there was a guy in the back stage area with a gun who was looking for me. Vernon was confronted by this man first. He told him that he was not his brother. My group members blocked the man from getting to me until security escorted the man out of the club. I later found out that he was the husband of the woman I had recently sexed up. She never mentioned that she was married, and I did not ask.

There was another time when our brotherhood was displayed. We were in Maryland in the dressing room preparing to perform, when we heard chairs crashing and bottles being broken. Ted runs into the dressing room and yells that" They are coming for us!" He then pointed to a big closet which was in the room and told us to get in there. We got in the closet and slammed the door. The noise that we heard was a gang fight in the club. Once that noise died down Ted went back to let us out of the closet. When he tried to open the door, he found out that it was locked. He could not open it from the outside and we could not open it from the inside. The door was made of metal and steel like a vault. No one in the club had a key. We could hear the crowd through the door yelling "Blue Magic, Blue Magic!" The club manager had to call a welder who came and opened the door with a torch. When we got out of that room, we quickly changed our clothes, and put on the show. I always appreciated Ted trying to protect the rest of the group during that incident.

Ted showed his protective nature another time when we were on the road travelling through Texas. The bus broke down in the desert. We had all kinds of drugs on us and some of us had just taken some PCP which is a hallucinogenic drug. The sun was setting. Ted stood up in the bus and told us that he heard that there were people who lived in the desert who hunt for people in situations like the one we are presently experiencing. Everyone stay in the bus, he told us, and I will go down the road watch out and protect us. When I woke up in the morning he was still sitting in the same spot. I never knew where Ted got the information about killers roaming the desert. Supporting his suspicions did not hurt. Ted's knowledge of Marshall Arts may have even given him the courage to feel that he could protect us. I was grateful.

Probably the situation that most exhibited our bond happened in Michigan. We performed another great show. We went to get something to eat in a restaurant before returning to the hotel. Along the way to the hotel after a good meal we were pulled over by the police. They were not very nice. Without any warning they pulled their guns and made all of us get out of the car and lie on the ground. Rick and I were sitting in the back of the station wagon and had trouble opening the rear door to get out. One of the cops got in the car and told us to" Get out or he was going to blow our brains out!" While laying on the ground we were searched and handcuffed. While I was being searched one of the officers ripped my pants. It was the middle of winter, there was snow covering the ground. It was extremely cold. The police did not give us a reason for the stop as they searched our car. Ted tried to ask one of the officers what did we do that justified us being made to lie on the ground? The officer responded by telling him to keep his face down on the ground. Ted was also concerned because he had three thousand dollars in his sock, that we just earned from the show we just performed. I thought, while on the ground in the dark that I was going to die as one of the officers kept pointing his gun at my head. They did not just have pistols they had shotguns. They did not find anything in our car so they had us get to our feet and walk about a mile to the local police precinct. While I was walking down the street I had to ask one of the officers to please pull my pants up as they kept falling down. This was a result of them being tore during the body search. Once in the precinct we were told that some girls in the restaurant reported seeing one of us with a gun. We now told them that we were the singing group Blue Magic. They did not initially believe us, if they even knew who we were. These were all white cops in the Midwest. Ted made his one phone call to Atlantic Records. The police chief came to the station within a short period of time. He asked his officers who we were? He then looked at us as we sat on a bench and said" So you guys are Blue Magic? My daughter has your records at home." I was shocked that he was familiar with our music because the chief was white. We were subsequently released.

That police stop was purely a racist move. An investigation of that situation determined that no one reported seeing any guns in our possession. We decided that we were not going to let that abusive behavior go. We filed a law suit against that Michigan Police Department.

We had two lawyers working for us on the lawsuit. During the deposition phase of the suit, we were called separately into a room to give our version of what happened. Our road manager Turk was called into the room first. He was followed by Rick then Keith, and then Vernon. I was never called. I figured that by the time they got to me there was no need to hear a repetition of what was stated by all the others. The suit was eventually settled in our favor.

Some years later a movie called "The Five Heart Beats" was on the big screen produced by and starring Robert Townsend. I thought that it was a good movie. It was said that the movie was loosely based on another popular singing group. I always felt that the characters portrayed in that movie were similar to members of our group. Even some the situations in the movie were the same as we experienced. First the Five Heart Beats had two brothers in the group. Vernon and I were a part of Blue Magic. There was a member of the Heart Beats who was the choreographer. He looked eerily like Keith Beaton, who created our dance steps. Keith and the movie character were both were of a light complexion and tall. When the group in the movie was stopped by the police and humiliated, that was us. Then there was the womanizer. That was me. The lead singer in the movie left the group. That was Ted. There was even a female character in the movie with the last name of Sawyer. In the movie the first time the brothers heard their song on the radio they were laying in bunk beds when their sister came into the room to tell them it was playing. This is exactly what happened to Vernon and I when our sister Lorraine came into our room, and told us that our song was being played on radio station WDAS in Philadelphia. I never met Robert Townsend but there were just many coincidences. I always felt that movie was our story.

We did a show somewhere in California, where after performing we went to a local Restaurant chain to eat. In the restaurant there were all white female waitresses. We travelled a great deal so that was not unusual. We sat down at a table and waited for service, that never came. Noticing that we were being ignored, I started chanting loudly "WE WANT SERVICE! WE WANT SERVICE!" What did I do that for? This scraggly looking guy came out from the back and reluctantly asked us what we wanted to eat. We all ordered after which he brings our food from the back of the restaurant. I started feeling queasy as I finished my meal. Vernon looked at me and told me that I was turning grey. I went into the bathroom and started violently throwing up. We had a plane to catch that same day, so although I felt sick, I was able to make it to the plane. Once we were seated on the plane Vernon got up and went to the bathroom. A couple minutes later we heard someone over the intercom requesting that the person in bathroom please return to his seat so that we could take off. Vernon struggles back to his seat and told me that he threw up all over the bathroom. Keith even got sick. My girlfriend at the time picked me up from the airport. On the way home she asked me what was wrong? Right after that question I made her pull over where I opened the car door and threw up again. I know that someone in that restaurant put something in our food that made us sick. They poisoned us. I guess they wanted to teach us niggers a lesson, which they did. We later heard that eating establishment was a favorite of the local Klu Klux Klan. That explained the cold reception we got when we entered the restaurant. The only reason we decided to eat there was because it was the only place open close to the hotel where we stayed. I would never, ever eat at one of the restaurants in that chain again in my life.

Racism reared its ugly head on us another time when we were scheduled to do a show in Frankfort Germany. When we checked into the hotel, we instantly received a cold reception from the desk clerk. He threw our keys at us and told us not to leave our rooms for any reason. Keith and I after dropping our bags in the room ignored his demands. We were hungry so we went back down to the lobby to inquire about getting some food. The desk clerk told us that nothing was open. I pointed to the restaurant on the premises where I saw people seated and eating. I was told that the restaurant was also closed. When we went back to our room we looked out of the window and saw many of the people who were in the restaurant leaving the hotel. We called our manager and told him that we needed to leave that hotel. He found another hotel for us that night.

On that same trip we had been advised to not stray too far away from each other. We were in a foreign country and an unfamiliar city. Vernon and Keith did not take that advice. They were invited by white German to her home. While sitting in the house a man opened the front door with key and looked at them and questioned who they were. He was told by the woman that they were friends and then he immediately left appearing to be angry. They realized that the decision to go home with this woman was a bad one. It could have ended badly.

The groups that were our rivals were The Futures, The Dynamic Superiors, and later the Stylistics. All due respect to these groups, but none of these groups could touch our stage show. The Futures only had one hit. The Dynamic Superiors, always did their best to outdo our group on stage. This group was out of Washington DC. Their lead singer really knew how to sing. We performed with them at Club Harlem in Atlantic City. We were the headliners so we performed last on the show. The crowd went wild clapping and yelling their names, at the end of their performance. One would have thought that they were the most popular singing group in America. When we came out and performed, people clapped at the end of our show but not with the enthusiasm that they showed for our opening act. We found out that our rival group had packed the audience with fans from their home of Washington.

CHAPTER 8
"ANSWER TO MY PRAYER"

We left WMOT in 1975 when our contract ended. We were not happy with the way we had been treated. We made money for the management company. They had an office located in downtown Philadelphia. Everyone was driving nice new cars and living the good life. During our episode of Unsung on television one of our managers mentioned that the cost of producing an album was thirty thousand dollars. Our first album sold over a million copies. All we received from that album was a check for sixty thousand dollars, to be split between the five of us. I wondered where did all the rest of the profits from the album go? We were making money on the road but I have no proof but still believe even there we were losing money. We knew nothing and were not taught anything about the business of music. We were taught nothing about publishing rights, or owning the masters from the songs that we recorded. I had to learn these things on my own. On some occasions we did ask management where all the money was going. We were always given the same type of answer that the money was being spent on travel, costumes, and to many miscellaneous expenses to mention them all. It was in the contract so we had no legal recourse. It reminded me of the advice we were given before we signed the contract. We did not take the advice. The opportunity to make money and possibly become famous was too much to turn down, for young men who had nothing. Ted's situation was a bit different because he was writer.

Ted was supposed to be our leader; however, every member of the group took the lead in some area. Ted found a man by the name of Erin Weiner who wanted to manage our group after we terminated our relationship with WMOT. Mister Weiner was a sports agent who represented Julius "Dr. J "Erving and basketball player Walt Frazier. We met Doc J in Mister Weiner's office on one occasion when he was with the Philadelphia 76'ers. He and his wife Turquoise were friendly and impressive.

We followed Ted's lead and decided to give the relationship a trial run. Erin Weiner was a nice guy. He flew us down to his home in Florida and set us up in a private villa. I guess he wanted to show us that he had the money to back our group. I was impressed with the first-class treatment we received, but all the time I was there I was thinking about whether he had the experience necessary to take care of managing a singing group. My experience in the business, although not a great deal, made me cautious. I felt we were in the driver's seat having had hit songs. I wanted to maximize our earning potential. Mister Weiner had no experience in the music business. He was a sports agent. We agreed to the relationship on a trial basis.

He sent his partner, who was white, to be our road manager. As the road managers usually did after each show, he collected our money. I walked out in the club area one night after changing in to my street clothes, and saw this road manager buying drinks for a bunch of black women at the bar. When I asked him, who was financing the drinks, he responded by telling me that he used some of the group's money. That answer made me angry. I then told him to never use our money for anything without our permission. I told Mister Weiner what happened when we got back to New York. To his credit he blasted the road manager for his behavior. A red flag went up in my mind after that experience with the money. I shared my concerns with Mister Weiner, about music business management. He responded by telling me that he had lawyers to handle my concerns. I then asked him to set up a meeting between the attorneys and our group. I did most of the talking during the meeting, as the rest of the group members did not say much. The Lawyers could not answer most of my questions to my satisfaction. They did not appear knowledgeable of the music business. I believed that since I was the member of the group, most concerned about how business was going to be conducted, Mister Wiener thought he could bring me into the fold by having us meet with his attorneys. It did not work. I shared my opinions on the matter with the other members of the group. I told them my conclusions were based on what I saw and heard. I questioned why the group did not see what I saw. We all had the same experience under our prior management. I understood why they did not want to entertain my concerns. They saw the money. We also saw the money and the opportunity when we signed our first contract with WMOT. A day or two later we went to Weiner's office where I refused to sign the contract. I, just did not feel that in the long run that contract was in our best interest." Fool me once shame on you, fool me a second time shame on me."

Richard Pratt and I got into a heated argument over my refusal to sign the contract we were offered. I noticed him turn the ring around on his finger as the argument escalated. We both threw up our hands and jumped into a boxing stance. I thought we were just playing around. We had disagreement before but nothing ever ended in a physical fight. Suddenly Rick punched me on the left side of my face just missing my eye. An ambulance was called and I was taken to a hospital. Three stitches were needed to close my wound. Vernon did come down to the ambulance to check on me before it pulled off. I later asked him why he did not have my back? He did not have an answer. I was so angry after being hit in the face and my brother not seeming to back me, that I remember while still in the hospital yelling something that was inarticulate. Rick never apologized for the punch in the face.

The very next weekend the group performed in New York without me. The day before the performance Vernon was driving down the Schuylkill Expressway, in Philadelphia, on his way home, when he was involved in an accident which landed him in the hospital. The group performed with only three members. The show I heard was a disaster. Vernon was fired because he missed the New York Show. People used to call my brother and I "the twins," even though we were a year apart. We did look alike. The Sawyer Brothers were the soul of Blue Magic. Our presence could not be duplicated. Mister Weiner did not want to work with a shorter version of the group. He wanted the five members in Blue Magic, that were responsible for all the hits records.

The remaining group members were invited to California to work on an album which was produced by Verdeen White the bass player for Earth Wind and Fire. The album did not do well. While they were in California, I tried talking to Ted, Rick, and Keith individually over the phone about rejoining the group. I had a change of heart. I hoped that they did. We had been through a lot together. There had been good times and bad times They did not want me back. I thought we were brothers. Brothers had disagreements, get mad at each other, and fought. Then they made up, forgave each other, and moved on. What hurt even more was Keith's rejection. When he was at one of the lowest points in his life, I took him in to live with me in my mother's home. I put Vernon on the phone and he was also rejected. I could not believe that Rick and Keith, who I grew up with could turn their backs on us. Their loyalty to friends from the old neighborhood was no longer there. Since Ted was the lead singer and the oldest member of the group, I thought that he was influential in persuading the other member of the group not to allow us back.

A month after, Vernon and I broke up with Blue Magic, I received a call from a man named Ozzie. He told me that his boss, a man by the name of Doctor York wanted Vernon and I to come to New York and audition for another group. Ozzie was Doctor York's business manager. He previously worked for Bob Marley and Peter Tosh. Vernon was still living at home with my mother. He might not have felt any pressure to find work and pay his bills. My situation was different. I explained to Ozzie that I wanted to come to New

York, but since I was not performing now, I did not have the funds to make the trip. I further explained that it was more important that I pay my bills and provide for my family. He sent Vernon and myself money sight unseen. I paid my bills and then I was ready for a trip to New York.

We took the train up to New York City, where we were picked up by a limousine. Ozzie was in the limo by himself. The car pulled around the corner after we got in and another man jumped in. To me this man looked a little strange. He introduced himself as Doctor Malachi York. He had a big afro hair style with a big part in it. This was the end of 1976. We were first driven to Bushwick Brooklyn, and shown his mosque on Hart Avenue. He then told us that now he wanted to take us to an apartment where we could stay. We were then driven to an area of the Bronx called Riverdale. I had never been in that area of the Bronx. It was very nice with tree lined streets.

We walked into the apartment where we going to stay, and I could not believe what I saw. I had never seen anything so plush. I had been in some nice houses and apartments but this place was beyond description in beauty. It reminded me of the type of place I envisioned a movie star might make his or her home. It was what I envisioned having one day. In the bedroom there was even a circular bed that rotated. The bar was fully stocked. There was also a downstairs living room. I was amazed! I was impressed. The next day we were picked up by Doctor York's right-hand man, named Wally. The limousine he was driving took us back to Brooklyn where the recording studio was located. The minute I met Wally,

I felt he did not like us. His facial expressions suggested a look as to say, "Who are these little niggers to deserve this treatment?" I think he also did not like to have to drive all the way from Brooklyn to the Bronx to pick us up. Doctor York was the lead singer in a group named Passion. He was looking to add some members to his group. We would rehearse with the other group members all day and then be driven back to Riverdale. We followed this routine for three or four days. On the third- or fourth-day Doctor York asked us to get behind the microphones and sing. When we finished singing he approached us. He had been monitoring the microphones as we sung. He told Vernon that he did not hear him singing. As result of that lack of performance he kept me and sent Vernon back to Philadelphia. I was now a member of the group Passion along with Mercelino, his last name I do not remember, Steven Wise, and Doctor York. I replaced a member of the group named Butch who passed away.

Although I was married and had two children by now, I stayed in New York to work with Passion. I then found out that everyone in the group was of the Islamic faith. I was eventually moved out of Riverdale and into one of the Muslim apartments, in Brooklyn. I had my own place which was in the middle of a Muslim community. I was not a Muslim, so my lifestyle was different from theirs. Occasionally I brought home female company. This was frowned upon by the Muslim brothers. It did not make me popular. What saved me was that Doctor York always loved Blue Magic's music and choreography.

We did most of our rehearsing at Doctor York's house. He lived at 715 Bushwick Ave in Brooklyn. His house was a mansion. He had a recording studio in his home. We rehearsed from eight in the morning until seven or eight at night. When we hit the stage, because of all the practice, our performances were flawless. I must admit that I learned a great deal about stage presence from this group. I rehearsed with Blue Magic but never to the extent that matched what I did with Passion. Doctor York had many of our stage outfits tailor made. Blue Magic never had tailor made suits, so this was a pleasant change. I thought that we were well dressed every time we hit the stage.

Doctor York loved the songs on the Blue Magic album that flopped. We sung some Blue Magic songs including some of those from the album that I did not participate in making. There were a couple of songs that Doctor York and I occasionally shared the lead. In one song we would battle over a female in the audience. That always went over well. We were always welcome there.

We basically performed in New York area club and venues. One of the places that I enjoyed performing was called "Brooklyn Two." We were always welcome there. On one occasion we did travel to Philadelphia where we did a show at the Blue Horizon Club. The Blue Horizon was in my old stomping grounds. It was only a few blocks from my mother home. I went with some of the group to her home for a nice visit where she told me how proud that she was of me. That was such a I good feeling.

While with Passion we went to see a Blue Magic show at the Apollo Theatre. I sat in the audience angry seeing two replacement guys performing my steps, and singing my parts on stage. Doctor York loved the group so much that on one occasion when we went to see their show in another venue, the van that was carrying the group broke down on the way to perform. Once it was announced that Blue Magic's transportation broke down and consequently would not be able to perform, he made a phone call to his Mosque. He then sent one of his trucks to pick up the group. He encouraged me to go along for the ride but I refused. That gesture was his way of trying to get me to forgive. I was hurt and angry because of how they treated me after so many years together. I was not ready to forgive.

Doctor York was not only the lead singer of the, he was also the leader of his Mosque. The Mosque's name was Anissa Allah "The Call of God." There were many Muslim Sects. The Sunni and Shite Muslims, were also strong in Brooklyn at the time. We all prayed to the same God but we had different philosophical beliefs. I eventually converted to Islam. During that time my wife and children came up to New York to visit me. While living in my apartment we were expected to follow tradition. Wendell Junior was even accepted in the Mosque and was given the Islamic name Salaam which meant "peace." That name fit my son because he was a peaceful soul. My wife could not take the lifestyle and decided that she wanted to move back to Philadelphia. That is what she did, moving in with her mother because we lost our apartment.

This was not the first Muslim group that tried to convince members of Blue Magic to join them. The Black Muslims sect led by Elijah Muhammad attempted to get us to join. We were part of a big show in an Armory in West Philadelphia, where we were approached by some Muslim Brothers. I knew nothing about Islam or Elijah Muhammad. There were Black Muslims all over the place in the building. I recognized them by their neat style of dress. I must admit that they were quite intimidating. Ted who was aware of their movement took three of them to the side and talked with them. I do not know what he said to them but they left us alone after that talk.

One day after returning to New York from visiting my family in Philadelphia I found that all my personal things were gone from my apartment. I asked some of the brothers in the Mosque what happened to my property? They responded by telling me that I now had to live in the Bayt which is the Islamic name for home. The Bayt that I was moved in to was a converted apartment building. I was assigned to an apartment with sixteen other men. The bunk beds were no more than three feet apart. They were so close together that my leg sometimes while sleep would cross into the bed next to mine. I had one drawer for my clothes. I was fortunate in that I did not have a lot. We were packed in this small apartment like sardines. I had a boom box so I could listen to my music. The brothers took it from me so that they could play Islamic music. On top of all that I had to pay rent which was twenty dollars a day. I knew the brothers in the Mosque were jealous because I spent so much time with Doctor York rehearsing. I was sure that they were influential in moving me out of Riverdale.

I was given an Islamic name upon my conversion. I thought it magical that while still living in Philadelphia one day I was reading the Bible, I turned the pages and stopped to read where my finger landed. The passage talked about Moses. I thought to myself that If I changed my name, I would like to be called Moses. I never knew how Doctor York came up with my Islamic name but he anointed me Musa Muhammad. Musa is Islamic for Moses. I never told anyone about my thoughts while reading the Bible on that one occasion. I kept that experience to myself, so when I found out Musa was Islamic for Moses it blew my mind.

I was taught to support myself and pay my rent by spending time on the subway trains pitching our cause. I did not want to do that but with the support of other Muslim brothers I learned the routine. The first time I went out I was wearing the traditional white Jelavia white outfit. I was able to make twenty dollars in a day easily, once I learned how it was done. The speech to the subway crowd went something like this. "Excuse me Ladies and Gentlemen we are from the Anssa Allah community. We are not government supported, so we need your support to keep the children that we have in school. If you could give a nickel, dime, or penny it would be appreciated." The first time I went out I was with Steve and Marceleno, both members of Passion. We usually would travel in pairs but my first time out it was the three of us.

One of the times while out I got a lesson in humility. I was walking down the isles between the seat in a subway car with my basket out to receive donations when a man looked at me and said that I did not need help because he noticed that I was wearing a nice diamond ring. I was embarrassed as I looked around the subway car and saw people looking at me with disgust. This was a good lesson for me to learn. I had been big time. Hell, I was a member of Blue Magic. I had been catered to as a member of that group. I heard someone tell me after I had gained success "Don't forget where you came from!" I must admit I forgot where I came from. I grew up poor, but while working with Blue Magic I made more money than I ever dreamed of making. Working forty- six weeks out of a year, and being idolized by my fans fed my ego. During those years I did not think about God, or anything that was not material. Getting embarrassed brought me back down to earth. That was a lesson learned.

I remember an occasion when the Sunni Muslims marched through our section of Brooklyn." Pop" we all affectionately called Doctor York came out into the street with a M16 rifle. He took this action to protect his followers and the neighborhood children. He was all about teaching and protecting the children. Doctor York knew that he was a target of law enforcement. I did not, until things started to happen when I was around him.

One evening he offered to drive my girlfriend Candy home, which we did. On the way back home, Pop decided that he wanted a pizza. He was sitting in the front passenger seat of the car his driver. I was in the back seat alone. His driver parked the car and crossed the street to the pizza parlor. Suddenly I noticed Pop quickly slide from the passenger seat over to the driver's seat and begin to pull our car behind the car in front of us. We were immediately cut off by a car that turned out to be a police vehicle. Cops seem to come from everywhere. Their guns drawn; they then pulled us out of the car. One cop pushed me to the side of the car and put his gun to the back of my head. That was the second time in my life that I had gun pressed against the back of my head. It is not a pleasant feeling. I did not know exactly what was going on? I did know that threats had been made against Doctor York's life. I thought now there was the possibility that I might die. Pop, who was bent over the hood on the opposite side of the car, made eye contact with me. I think that he sensed my fear. He had to see it in my eyes. Then in a respectful but stern voice, he told the police that he was a minister and a teacher. He explained where we came from and where we were going. It was astonishing when they just let us go. Doctor York's driver stood across the street the whole time this incident was taking place. I later found out that Doctor York waved him off from coming across the street. I struggled with understanding why people would want to take someone's life just for speaking out loud their thoughts and feelings. I knew Martin Luther King Jr and Malcolm X were killed for speaking the truth but at the time I did not connect those assassinations and the type of men that they were. It took some time for me to understand the power of words.

There was another time when that I went along with Doctor York, his driver and two other brothers to Philadelphia. Our purpose for the trip was to visit the Anssa Allah Mosque located in that city. There were rumors that the

Imam in that Mosque was not performing in a way that could be admired. While staying in a hotel, my roommates Steve, Mercelino and I went to visit Pop in the room he shared with his driver. We knocked on the door. They had to then remove all the furniture in the room from in front of the door to let us in. When we entered the room, I noticed the driver had possession of a 357-magnum pistol. It was these types of situations that let me know the danger that Pop faced.

Doctor York was more influential on my thinking than any other person that I had ever met. He taught me his philosophy about life. I had never had anyone take as much time with me as an individual. He challenged me to think. He taught me more about music than anyone who I was involved with in Blue Magic. He sent me to a vocal coach. She was also involved with his Mosque. He taught me simple things like how you should hold a microphone to get the best effect. He suggested ways to look sexy when performing; and what you should do on stage when you are the lead singer. I never learned any of the things that he taught me while I was with Blue Magic. We taught ourselves for the most part. He talked about projecting on stage. He taught me how to interact with the audience. These things were important to entertaining. Pop and I became so close that I would have taken a bullet to protect him. We even began to look so much alike that young children would sometimes mistake me for him because of our similar style of dress.

Another thing that I admired about Doctor York was his willingness to engage me in a debate concerning religion. The other group members I thought were intimidated or scared to question him. I was not. To his credit he never seemed to take my questions as an attack on what he preached. I admired the fact that he was sensitive. He cared about black people. He was concerned about where the African American race was headed. He wrote a book called Revelations. We had many discussions about the content in that book.

Our band was made up of all Muslim musicians. Between the singers and the musicians there were twelve of us like the twelve disciples of Christ. Doctor York was number thirteen. Many of the brothers in the Mosque were jealous of the group and band because we spent so much time with him. I was with him from morning to night. During our times together he took every opportunity to educate me to his way of thinking about religion and the world. Doctor York told me that his great grandfather was Al Ma Hadid. Al Hadid, he believed was close to Muhammed.

Life in the Mosque was totally structured. It was a rule that if you left the Mosque you had to tell someone that you were going out. You also had to tell one of the brothers when you would return. I got permission one time to visit my family in Philadelphia for Christmas. I was told that I could stay three days. I stayed a week. I heard upon returning that Doctor York was asking about me after the three-day period ended. That was only natural since we spent so much time together. It was said that he was concerned that I might be dead because members of one Mosque had been known to kidnap a member of another Mosque. I spoke with Doctor York upon my return and tried to explain my behavior. I just wanted to spend time with my family. I missed my children. He did not say anything to me, he just walked away.

In the Mosque there was an organization that was considered our police. They were called, Mujahid. Awhile after Doctor York walked away, I went to the Bayt where I lived. Six members of Mujahid showed up. One of them hit me in the stomach an another smacked me so hard in the face that it pushed me across the room. The slapper then told me not to do that again! I was embarrassed, more than hurt. Once they left, I walked up the street to a local pay phone. Standing by the phone I saw all six men scatter in different directions. I guess they were worried about who I was going to call. I did not call anyone; I was just mad. On top of it all when I went back to the Bayt, I had no bed. They took my bed away so I subsequently had to sleep on the floor for a period. I was also told that there was a rat that ran around on the floor at night. I still accepted my punishment.

A year passed and I began to get homesick. One day I got a call from Vernon telling me that my money from our lawsuit was ready to be picked up. Upon hearing that news, I felt it was time for me to go. I made the decision to give up the group and that whole lifestyle. It was time for me to move on. I thought that I had learned what I needed to continue to advance in my life. Getting that money gave me the independence to go back home. Life in that Mosque became too structured for me. Everyone had to get up at 4 AM for morning prayers in the Mosque. By the time you returned to the Bayt, where we lived it was time to go out in the street to solicit money. We had to pray five times a day. In some ways that was good. It kept Allah on our minds every day, but I was tired of all the structure. I likened leaving with

Jesus going into the poorest neighborhoods to preach and help. I convinced myself that I was going back home for the same reason. It was a good rational even if it was not totally true.

The day I left I tried to sneak out of the building by leaving at 6 AM. As I walked down the street, I saw Doctor York standing in front of his house. He never got up that early. He somehow knew that I was leaving. I told no one what I was planning. I made advance plans with my father to pick me up at a Laundromat nearby. I always wondered how he knew. I always felt that he had special powers and insight. That insight always made me cautious when I left the house.

When I relocated back to Philadelphia, I moved into the second floor of my mother in law's house where my wife, daughter, and son already lived. I set up shop in the basement, hanging my clothes on pipes and trying to make the basement mine. During this period of time, I must admit that I began again to smoke a lot of reefers. I had been drugged free for the better part of a year. Moving back into my old neighborhood was enough motivation for me to pick up old habits. Terrible as it sounds, I would read the Koran while high. During this time, I was also introduced to a nice young lady through my sister. She was good to me, so I started sneaking over to her house. One day my mother-in-law came down into the basement, and jumped in my ass, with complaints about me hanging my clothes on the pipes. She felt, and rightfully so, that the weight of the clothes would break the pipes. Since I was not happy with how I lived, and where I lived, I used that as an excuse to leave. I moved in with my sister's friend.

That is how I left my wife. I was wrong. I should not have left, but between smoking reefer and people whispering in my ear, I was looking for an escape. It did not help that I was living in someone else's home, where I had no control. Some of my thinking at that time I blame on my use of marijuana again. I had been practicing the faith of Islam in New York not so long ago. I had been taught to do the right thing. Living a righteous life was constantly preached. I was now going against all those teachings, by back sliding into my old negative behavior.

I did not really think things through before I moved because my new roommate had six children. I tried being a substitute father at times while neglecting my own children. It did not work out well. I did not have much contact with my wife or Shemeka after I moved. I did see Wendell Junior who was now around twelve years old. He sought me out and kept our relationship going. It is painful even now to talk about the lack of a relationship that I had with my daughter. I always thought that father daughter relationships were special. I failed at my job of protecting Shemeka. During this period, I met another young woman at my mother's house that I found very attractive. She was a friend of my two younger siblings. We started dating and she eventually got pregnant with my daughter Tinesha. In later years Shemeka found out that I fathered a sister by her friend. She was already bothered by how I had treated her mother over the years. I am sure that this added to her questionable feelings about me. I do not blame her my behavior was wrong and irresponsible.

Our relationship is much better today although I think

that she still has some resentment. That resentment which I understand. I only hope for as much forgiveness as she is willing to give.

Approximately seven years later after I moved back to New York. I asked my wife at that time if I could have back my gold albums. She had taken possession of them when she moved from our apartment to her mother's home. I had three gold records single songs, and one gold album. I thought she was still angry with me behind for the way I left her and the children. She told me that she could not find them. I think that even if she knew where they were, she would not have given them to me. I cannot blame her. I was a bad person, with a poor sense of responsibility. I never saw those gold records again.

CHAPTER 9
"CHASING RAINBOWS "

The drug world is a hard world! Drugs were everywhere in my neighbor. The first drug I used was reefer. I experimented with drugs even before becoming a part Blue Magic. The one drug that made an early impression on me, around the time that I started performing was called "Tack." It was a powder like cocaine which you snorted. Tack burned your nose once you snorted it, but we could rehearse for hours while under its Influence. It had to be a form of speed. I did not know what was in the drug but I used it anyway. I admit that was not very smart. Everywhere that we went on the road drugs were always available. I remember going into a club after hours in New York where cocaine was visible on tables. No one seemed to be worried about the police. It was sad but drugs legal and illegal were a part of the culture when I got into the music business.

I did a show once after taking a tablet of acid. It was the worst thing that I could have ever done. Everyone in the group did a quarter tab, I did a whole one. When I ran out on stage it appeared that everyone in the audience was looking at me, like they knew I was high. This made me paranoid. My microphone appeared to be oversized and moving away from me. I was hallucinating so bad that I ran off stage. I then tried talking to myself. "Come on Wendell get it together!" I got myself together well enough to go back on stage and finish the show. I cannot even count the numbers of times that I used hallucinogenic drugs. Ted had an oil which he would use, and he rubbed on our heads. I never knew what it was. He told us it was holy oil. Ted never explained the purpose of the oil. We trusted him so we did not question what it was. We rubbed it on our heads. I can only suspect it was not a drug. There was no intoxicating effect from rubbing on our heads. His reason for doing it was probably something spiritual. He was a very spiritual person.

We bought our drugs from a select number of dealers. We would not buy from just anyone. There was a club in West Philadelphia, where I could always get what I wanted.

When we first became the new Blue Magic none of us were using cocaine. We really could not afford it. That was the rich man's drug. One of the strangest experiences I had with drugs early in my career was in the Jamaica, West Indies. We bought a pound of Marijuana while we were there for our personal use. We had so much weed that we were rolling joints out of large newspapers and smoking them. When we checked out of the hotel, we left weed all over the room. We landed back at Philadelphia International Airport, picked up our bags from the carousel and went to our homes. The next day on the television news it was reported that on that same carousel three suspicious bags had not been picked up. When the authorities opened the bags, they were full of marijuana. We tried to figure out whose bags did they belong too. We thought that it was someone from management. They got high just like we did. Maybe once we landed whoever brought the bags back thought that it was risky to pick them up so they just left them.

I had a friend who was also a cocaine dealer. He lived in the Newark, New Jersey area. He invited the whole group to his house one evening. He was a big fan. Once we got to his place, he told us that he was going to get some drugs so that we could get high. Returning home sometime later he poured a pile of cocaine on a table. We were all past using powdered cocaine, we liked to smoke crack which was then called 'free basing!" We started cooking up the cocaine; turning it into a rock form that we could put in a pipe and smoke. We repeated this process over and over. Everybody was getting high except the ladies, who were with us. We smoked all night. Around 5 o'clock in the morning, we heard a noise outside. I peeked through the blinds and saw cops everywhere. They had surrounded the house next door. There was no one home in that house so after searching the police left. As luck would have it, they went to the wrong house. If they had raided the residence we were in, it would have been over for us. We had so many drugs and drug paraphernalia in the house that all of us would have gone to jail.

The worse drug by far that I ever used was crack cocaine. I was introduced to this drug by my brother and our drummer. They took me over to New Jersey and told me what they were going to do. I gave them money to get me powdered cocaine and did not want mine used in any other way. I watched them pour all the cocaine into some water which meant that I could not snort it. I was pissed off. They did not have my permission to use my twenty dollar worth that way. I was so angry that I wanted to fight. They convinced me to be cool. I then watched them cook up all the powdered cocaine until it crystallized. They put the rocks in a pipe and told me to take a hit. I took a pull on the pipe and I did not feel anything. Now I am really pissed. I was not high but they were. Although I did not get high, I was curious enough that on another occasion I tried it again. The next time I did get high. That was the beginning of the beast. It took me down a road I wish I had never gone. I lost countless amounts of money and wasted years because of that drug. Dorothy from the Wizard of Oz followed the yellow brick road to the" Poppy Fields" I followed that same road to the world of crack cocaine.

Crack became the worst enemy I ever faced. It was worse than poverty, gangs, or police abuse. Once I started smoking, I basically spent all the money that I had to get it. What made things worse was that I was working, so dealers had no problem extending me credit. I was living in a Co-op Building in Queens New York that was full of dealers. I did not have to go far to look for what I wanted. One dealer lived right down stairs under me. All I had to do, like any other crack head, was to come up with the money. I was living with young woman at the time who had performed in the movie "The Wiz" starring Diana Ross and Michael Jackson. She never used any drugs beyond weed until I turned her on to crack. Once she tried some she was hooked.

I met her one night while performing at a club across the street from her apartment. At the time I was living with Joyce in Philadelphia. We were scheduled to perform two shows, one on Friday night and the other on Saturday night. The group was going to take the ride back home after the

Friday show and would return to New York for the Saturday Show. I saw her sitting at one of the tables in the club and I thought she was beautiful, which she was. I approached her after the show and struck up a conversation. When the evening ended, she invited me back to her apartment. I decided to stay in Queens and meet the group at the club the next night. Some of my group members including the two sons of my current paramour, who were working with us, frowned on my decision. I did not care. I did what I wanted right or wrong. When I arrived at her place, she introduced me to her mother and daughter. We stayed up all night talking.

Meeting her came along at the right time. A short time later I found out that my Philly paramour was cheating on me. Her infidelity resulted in her giving me a venereal disease. This made it easy for me to do what I wanted to do. I packed up my bags and moved to New York and in with her.

I tried to hide my use from my new love but eventually she wanted to know what I was doing. Telling her that I did not think that smoking crack was something that she wanted to experience, made her even more curious. She was never into drugs beyond some weed but once I turned her on, she was hooked just like me. One time while using I did something stupid beyond belief. I wanted some crack but had no money so I used my platinum Blue Magic album with Big Daddy Kane as collateral. The agreement was that the dealer would return my album when I paid him what was owed. This agreement worked several times. That agreement finally went sour. When I went to pay him, and retrieve my property he gave me some bad news. He told me that he had a fire in his apartment and my album was destroyed. That album was given to him in trade for forty dollars of crack. I was never able to prove it but I believe that he decided to keep my album. He gave me the information about the fire at his front door, and never let me inside to see the alleged damage. That was just one instance when I did something stupid to get high. Even though he probably ripped me off, my addiction to crack was so powerful that I continued to do business with him.

There was another area close to where I lived in South Jamaica Queens that I could walk to and buy crack. During this period there was a war against drugs going on in the neighborhood between the drug dealers and the police. The police had a special task force dedicated to this war. They were called "TNT" which stood for Tactical Narcotics Team. They would set up surveillance on areas where drugs were sold and pick off the buyers one by one. Once they made enough arrests of the buyers, they arrested as many dealers as they could and close the locations down. The dealers who were not arrested of course just moved to a new location. Knowing that situation, I still was willing to take the risk to get high.

On one occasion I walked to a corner that was familiar to me to buy some crack. I purchased three or four vials and, got about half a block away when a police officers in plain clothes approached me. Before they searched me, I heard over one of their police radios "That's not him, it was the other guy!" They immediately jumped back in their car and drove back to where I bought the drugs. If they had searched me, they would have found the crack I just bought. This was another example of me dodging a bullet while involved in the drug world.

I was embarrassed many times when I went to purchase crack. The embarrassment was not enough to stop me. I was a member of the famous singing group Blue Magic. In my mind I felt that I was above the kind of behavior associated with crack heads. That was what I told myself but I bought the drugs anyway. I had a dealer refuse to sell to me because he said that I was too nicely dressed. I saw how the crack heads around me acted and looked. I found some of their personal hygiene discussing. I tried to carry myself differently. All I really was doing was fooling myself, because I still bought the drugs.

Crack contributed to the destruction of my relationship with my live in lover. We broke up after constant arguments over drugs after several years together. It is unbelievable that we lasted as long as we did. We were truly crack heads. It was so bad that on one occasion she believed that I stole her crack before leaving our apartment. She called the police, and told them that I stole her property. I was standing on the Long Island Railroad platform across the street from our place when she approached me with two police officers. "There he is" she yelled, as she pointed me out to the officers. I was carrying a shoulder bag. I denied having stolen anything from her, so I gave her permission to search my bag. What I could not believe was that she was going through my bag in front of the police looking for crack. If I did have her drugs, in my bag, we were both getting arrested. When I came back home later that day, I found the crack rocks, that she had been looking for in between the cushions in the living room sofa. It really got crazy living with her.

The drug use seemed to have changed her from the sweet person that I originally met to a paranoid person with different personalities. Our group was interviewed by Disk Jockey Shala on The WBLS radio station in New York. Shala and I got along fabulously during the interview. I thought we made a connection. Before I left the studio, she gave me her telephone number. I am not sure when my girlfriend found the number written on a piece of paper. She did not say anything right away. Later we were riding in her car when while she was driving, she leaned over and just started hitting me without warning. I did not know what was going on until she asked me, while at the same time hitting me, why did I have Shala's number? She was not only punching me but her daughter who was in the back seat pulled off her shoe and was also trying to hit me in the back of the head. Her daughter was only seven or eight years old at the time. I could not take the attacks so when the car slowed down because of the traffic I jumped out of the vehicle. She drove off leaving me on the highway. I managed to walk off the highway into what appeared to be a Puerto Rican neighborhood. I was not in familiar surroundings, and I had very little money on me. Using crack kept me broke. While walking I heard some of the residents talking about what they should do to me, since I was not from the neighborhood. I found a pay phone where I called my friend Khalid who came and picked me up.

Khalid and I first met when he also sang with Doctor

York. He tried to replace Doctor York as the lead singer of his group. He became one of my closest friends. As luck would have it when I moved to New York this second time, Khalid lived a couple of blocks from me. When my lady friend and I would get into one of our crazy fights, I went to Khalid's home.

I have had four close friends who influenced my life. First there was Ronnie Stubbs. We met when he moved into my neighborhood and was first friendly with my neighbor across the street named Bobby. Our friendship developed from our horsing around in our early teens. By the time that we entered high school we were best friends. Our trust was such that we could tell each other anything. Our friendship faded over the years as I moved away from where he lived. The other two close friends were Keith, from Blue Magic, Doctor York.

The person that I lived with became so crazy that she started hallucinating. I came into the bedroom one night to go to sleep when she woke up jumped on my back and accused me of screwing a woman in our living room, which was not true. I figured that she was dreaming and was unable to distinguish between the dream and reality. She was really strung out. She would take her daughter who was six or seven into the bathroom with her and smoke. She was hiding the drugs from me but smoking in front of her daughter. We both neglected her daughter to the point that when she was fourteen years old, we would leave her at home alone with her boyfriend. The result of that neglect of course was that she got pregnant.

I did not stop using crack until I broke up with my girlfriend and moved away from the neighborhood where I lived. I realized at some point that I needed to leave or either end up dead or in jail. I believe that had my life's direction been different, had I lived in a nicer neighborhood, during my formative years or had I been exposed to a different lifestyle, I probably would have never used drugs. I was the oldest of my parent's children so I had to learn many things by trial and error. Sometimes those errors were devastating, or at least led me in the wrong directions. I think in many cases my substance use was more situational than addictive.

I am proud to say that I have not used any illicit drugs in the past twenty years. It does bother me that I sometimes have a drink of brandy at night to get to sleep. The only addictive substance that even now I cannot kick is cigarettes. I still smoke a pack a day. I cognitively know that smoking cigarettes is bad for me but I cannot stop. I admit that I have never sought help to stop. It is no secret that cigarette companies have targeted menthol cigarettes towards black community. I have smoked menthol cigarettes for years. I guess I am a victim of nicotine and their advertising.

I must admit that at this point in my life I do not eat properly. I do not have an appetite some days, and that bothers me. I feel that is a problem.

CHAPTER 10
"THE LONELIEST HOUSE ON THE BLOCK"

During the time when I finally came to some realization of what I was doing to my body using drugs, I met a young lady. I met her in the same club in Queens, where I met my current girlfriend. She was sitting at the same table where I met my paramour. That night after my show I approached her and we began talking. I asked her for her phone number before she left the club that evening. She was first reluctant to give it to me but she finally gave in. I started calling her, and calling her, to point that she asked me why the continuous calls. I told her that I enjoyed talking to her. I thought she that she and had a sexy West Indian accent. She was the exact opposite of my current girlfriend. She did not smoke, drink, or use drugs. I knew soon after some of talks that I needed to be around someone like her to achieve sobriety. I also knew that I needed to move out of the neighborhood where I lived. I had been getting high my whole adult life. She was a respite from my old self. I now began to like the new Wendell when I was around her. It took me until I was in my fifties to really get to know and be comfortable with myself. I started dating her in secret while still living with my current girlfriend.

What finally brought my relationship to and end happened when her brother got on a bus that I happened to be on with my new friend and her two children. He saw us together, and consequently went right to his sister and told her what he saw. I would not have handled that situation that way but I was not him. His sister went ballistic. I could no longer keep my relationship with that new love a secret. It was time for our eleven-year relationship to end. It should have ended before then but it did not. My biggest regret in that relationship was that I turned her on to crack cocaine.

My sister-in-law told me about an apartment that she and her sister had vacated and she still had the keys. She told me that for the time being I could live there. I moved there by myself. Prior to my breaking up, my new girlfriend also had problems with her landlord. I had previously set it up for her to rent out my friend Khalid's basement apartment. She and her children had been residing there for about a year when she got in to an argument with Khalid's wife and had to move again. I then invited her to live with me in my apartment which was rent free. That was the first place where we lived together. We had been living there for about two years when we were finally discovered. Men were working in the hall and heard noise in the apartment one day when I was home. They knocked on the door and I did not answer it. They then used a drill and punched out the lock and confronted me about being in the apartment. When my paramour came home from work, I told her that we had to move. There was a hotel down the street from where we were living. We moved in there and paid rent while we looked for an apartment. We did find a place in Brooklyn. Two years later my youngest daughter Crystal was born on March 19, 2002.

Once I moved out of my old girlfriend's apartment, I wanted to get the clothes and the personal articles that I left behind. I decided to call her mother and ask for her help in retrieving my things. She had always been a buffer between the two of us when we had a fight. Her mother's advice to me was not go anywhere near her daughter. She warned me that she thought she was dangerous. That warning reminded me of an incident where we were fighting in the bathroom. During the fight she yelled to her daughter to bring her a butcher knife from the kitchen, which she did. I realized then that she was prepared to kill me. Whenever she threatened to kick me out, I would pack a bag go and stay with my friend Khalid, just for that reason. Over time I started moving my things to his basement. This made my moving transition much easier later.

There came a time when the mother of my youngest child, messed up her money and we got behind paying our rent. I did not know that there was a rent problem until it was too late for me to do anything about it. I was traveling and performing so I expected her to handle some of our bills.

When we got evicted from our Brooklyn apartment, we moved to my father's home in Hempstead, Long Island. My dad lived alone and had a room in his house where we all slept. When I say all slept, I meant three children and two adults. It was tight but we were trying to save money so that we could again get our own place. The most serious problem we had cohabitating with my father was that he was telling people that we were having sex in the bedroom while the children were sleeping. I found out about this slur from a cousin that he told this to. I was furious after hearing this story. I was far from perfect but I would never do anything as careless as that. The older children were not babies, they were six and seven years old. I told my lady friend what I heard. Why did I do that? She went into the living room with steam coming out of her ears and blasted my father who was sitting in his easy chair. She chastised him for saying something that scandalous. When I saw how she berated him I knew we were going to have to move again.

To try and mediate what happened, my dad invited the pastor of his church to his home to talk with all of us. I thought this was a good idea knowing that what my father had done was purely evil and totally wrong. I was sure that this pious man would point out to my dad the era of his ways. To my surprise the pastor did just the opposite. He ignored my father's behavior and defended him. He told us that he thought that we should move. I figured out that my father, a deacon in his church, gave seriously large amounts of money to his place of worship. There was no way that pastor was going to cut off the money from the golden goose. Finances took precedence over what was right. Religion as a business showed its ugly face.

There was another time, before we moved, when my father's car broke down and had to be repaired, so he had to rent a car. I went with him for support to get the rental car. He gave the car rental company permission to put me down as a driver on the car and the insurance. I came to him one day while he still had the rental car and told him that I was going to use the car to travel to a rehearsal in Brooklyn. He shocked me when he denied my request. He told me that he thought that all I was going to be doing was driving around and smoking reefer in the car. Sadly, he did not believe that I was going to a rehearsal. I did not use marijuana or any other drugs while in my father's house. He was aware of my history with drug use. I guess in his mind he felt that I had not changed. I tried to explain to him that I did not use drugs anymore. He did not believe me. This exchange reminded me of the way he treated me as a child. He would allow my brother Vernon to do things with him that he would not allow me do. He would always tell me that I was too much like my mother. I always felt, even as a child, that he resented me. I never knew what made him feel that way or why? I do know that he was selfish, in so many ways.

While living with my father he wanted me to attend a barbecue at the home of a friend also living in Long Island. He told me it would be a chance for me to meet my older brothers. Vernon also attended this event where we met them and had some very nice conversations. This was the first time that we met our brothers. They told us how proud they were of our success, which was a good feeling. The awkward part of the picnic was that my mother was also in attendance along with the mother of my older brothers. I could tell that my mother was not happy. My father seemed oblivious to the situation. There was a rumor that my half-brother's mother kicked him out of the house after he was caught cheating on her. My older siblings did come and visit my father in his waning years before his death. I have stayed in contact with them over the years.

My paramour had a friend at work, who knew someone that had an apartment for rent in the Hempstead area. I met with the owner whose family also lived in the same residence. We were able to rent the apartment. My daughter was able to attend a nursery school right down the street from our new residence. We got behind in the rent again. She once again messed up our money, failing to pay some of the bills. It took time but I finally figured out that she was a poor money manager. We agreed that she would use her money to catch up on our back rent, and I would take over from there. She was expected to pay the back rent once she received her tax return refund. Instead of following through on the agreement she sent all the money from her tax refund to her mother in Guyana who was suffering as the result of a tsunami. I felt sorry for her mother but our family also needed a place to live. She cried telling me that her mother was in trouble which was why she had to help. I angrily responded that she may have helped her mother's financial problems but we were now in trouble ourselves.

The owner of the property sent her daughter to collect the rent or evict us. Her husband accompanied his wife on this visit. I knew we had to move, because now we far behind on our rent. I started packing up my possessions in boxes, in anticipation of the move. When they arrived, while talking to us, the husband acted like he was carrying a gun in his pocket. He stood by the door while his wife confronted us. I could smell the alcohol on her breath as she stood in front of me. I thought she was drunk. I told her that I knew that we had to move and asked for more to time to pack. "I want you out now!" She demanded. When we refused to leave immediately, she called the cops. The officers who arrived assessed the situation and told her that she could not throw us out the way she wanted. They even told her that they thought that she was drunk and after some verbal battling, they told her to leave before they locked her up. On her way out of the residence she kicked a box full of my things down the steps. My live- in girlfriend suggested that we move into her ex-husband's apartment temporarily. I had visited his place in the past. He had one bedroom a living room and a kitchen. I could not do that. I lied and told her that I was going back to live with Khalid. I did not want to put that type of pressure on him again but that is what I told her. That was the end of our cohabiting together. I really wanted to make things work between us, if nothing else but for the sake of my daughter. I was now fifty years old and had never been there for any of my other children's births. I also did not raise any of them. I wanted this time to be different. The fifty years old me was different from the twenty years old me. Maturity has its benefits. She was just terrible with money, and as a result we kept getting into financial holes. I hated moving but once again we had no choice. She moved in with her ex-husband. I moved in with a friend named Carol.

I met Carol through a friend who managed the "34TH Street Bar." The bar was located inside of the Manhattan Center, where I worked part time when I was not performing. Carol and I became friends during this association and I found out that she was interested in managing a music group. During one of our conversations, I told her that she always looked miserable. I was trying to loosen her up because I thought she was a nice person. She was collecting the money at the door when customers came to the bar. I thought a pleasant personality would help as she greeted people. Our friendship developed from our association at the bar. Carol's strongest attribute was her understanding of finance. She was the total opposite of my youngest child's mother when It came to money. I made the decision for the group to use her talents. The group needed an organized manager and she wanted to work in the music industry. It was a perfect match at that time. She took control of Blue Magic's direction with my guidance. I told her what booking agents and promoter that she should contact. She even helped us trade mark our name. She was very helpful and seemed to enjoy what she was doing.

Carol's weakness was her jealousy. Being an entertainer, women were always approaching me. It was good public relations to be friendly. Sometimes Carol would turn into another person when she saw me talking to them or a woman touching me. I eventually had to sit down and explain to her that I was going home with her every night after I performed, but that I could not turn my back or be snobbish towards my fans. I had seen other artist treat their fans badly. I refused to treat people who enjoyed my music that way. We were able to work out her feelings about that situation. We were together for the next fifteen years. Unfortunately, we also broke up. Carol wanted to get married and so did I. The problem was that I was already married. She invested in a beautiful wedding dress and bought us nice wedding bands only to find out that my ex-wife refused to grant me a divorce. I owned a small piece of land which I originally wanted to give to Wendell Junior. I made a gentlemen's agreement with my daughter Shemeka who was handling her mother's affairs to sign over the property in exchange for her granting me a divorce. That was a mistake. I should have used an attorney to make the agreement because she reneged on the agreement and I lost possession of the land. Carol eventually just got tired of all the legal maneuvering. I do not blame her for that. I do miss the time we spent together going out to dinner and talking among the many enjoyable things that we did.

My old girlfriend is still alive and residing in Philadelphia. We were together for seven years. We occasionally talk to each other. The woman with which I cohabitated in New York currently lives in Virginia. I heard that her daughter moved to the Texas. The mother of my youngest daughter and I talk regularly. She is still a nomad moving from place to place. I guess old habits never change. As I tell this story I realized that we moved at least four times while we were together. My daughter Crystal has turned into a beautiful young lady recently graduating from high school. We talk often.

CHAPTER 11
"THREE RING CIRCUS"

Besides the music business being vicious and cut throat, it was also naturally very competitive. Egos were flying all over the place. The singing group Black Ivory had their first hits a year or so before us. I went to the Uptown Theatre in Philadelphia to see them perform. I was a fan. I even went backstage and got their autographs. I never dreamed that I would ever perform with them. It did happen after we had a hit record. During the show with them I witnessed members of the group backstage loudly questioning the promoter as to why our group was going on stage after them. They complained that because they had been around longer, they deserved to be given that respect. This attitude reminded me of our experience with Ike Turner. The promoter tried to explain to them that Blue Magic now had the big records. Years later while talking to Stuart Bascom, a member of Black Ivory, he admitted that they were pissed because we got a top billing on that show.

We were in the Virgin Islands sharing the stage with a popular singing group. Two shows over two nights. The first night we went on stage first, followed by this talented group. We did not have a problem with that decision. They had been around a long time and we were relatively new to the business. The second night the promoter decided that he wanted our group to follow them. Members of their group went ballistic. It was their feeling that they had been around so much longer, so they should perform last. The promoter diplomatically explained to them that Blue Magic was so polished on stage, with their choreography, and their ability to interact with the crowd that he had no choice. He felt our stage show was better. The star act usually got paid more. On that show this group was the star act. When we changed positions with them, we should have gotten a bump up in our pay but we did not. We honored our contract. What that performance did was improve our status as R&B artists. We never minded going on stage first. It meant if you followed our act you had to work harder to outdo what we gave the crowd. Rather than help and support their fellow artist I found some to be critical not constructive.

I thought that there were some famous bands and singing groups who were arrogantly out of their minds! When we went to greet them backstage the first time we met, they treated us like dirt. One band as they passed us, would not speak or even acknowledge that we existed. Yes, they had been on the music scene longer with a few hit records, but there was no reason to treat us with disdain. We were fellow entertainers. I felt that their egos were out of control. I also did not think that it was good for the music business in general.

Witnessing that type of behavior from some performers made me vow to never be that way. I wanted others to achieve the success that I had attained. I witnessed some artists refuse to simply sign an autograph for a little child. For a kid or anyone else to walk up to you and ask for your autograph was a compliment. I wondered did these artists ever wonder what that meant to that person. I saw it as an honor to give someone my signature. I always thought that if your ego caused you to treat fellow artists or fans with no respect what did that say about you as a person.

There were entertainers who were not ego tripping. Gladys Knight and the Pips were one such group. Although they were big stars they were down to earth people. They were special. We did our first show at the Westbury Music Fair, in Long Island New York with them. It was a theatre in the round with a stage that rotated as you performed. We did not know how to maneuver on stage as this was a new situation. Bubba Knight suggested what he thought we should do on the stage. It worked perfectly. We were grateful for his advice.

Singer and composer Isaac Hayes was a gentleman and a person who treated us as equals. He was as popular a performer as anyone. He was a real brother. There was no pretense about him. When we met him, it was like we had known him for years. He explained to us that the chains that he wore around his neck were given to him by an African tribe that made him a king. He was a true superstar but you would not have known it.

The Spinners were another inspiration to our group. They performed the song "One of a Kind" during their show with us. Their interactions with the crowd were so electric, that at the end of the song, at the audience request they did the song again. They repeated the whole song again! When have you ever seen that done in a live performance? We were students soaking up everything that we could absorb. We watched and learned.

On the Mike Douglas television show we performed along with Sammy Davis Jr. We sang "Side Show." There was a point in the song, where we quickly went back stage and put on clown suits to finish the act. That act was Influenced by the Spinner's" One of a Kind" actions. We did not know that Sammy was on the show until we saw him in front of the cameras performing "Candy Man." As we left the studio at the end of the show, we passed Sammy in the hallway. His first response after greeting us was to say "You all are some sharp brothers!" This was a great compliment coming from Sammy Davis Jr. It meant a lot to us. We always wore suits and ties like business men when we were together before the pubic. No sweat suits or jeans were seen on Blue Magic during that time. We felt that the black man in this country had been looked down on so long so we wanted to present a different image partly through our dress.

We opened a show for Richard Pryor in Washington D C. While on stage we heard Richard applaud our performance by saying to the audience. "Did you see those brothers? Their steps on stage were great!" That was respect from one of our peers. We also did a show where Eddie Murphy opened for us. This was before he really blew up. Sometime later we saw him on the Jay Leno show where he praised us and talked about us not getting paid after our show. He made a joke, as only Eddie could do, out of how the little guy in our group was really pissed off. He was talking about Ted.

Mick Jagger of the Rolling Stones was another artist with which we collaborated. The connection with our group was because WMOT management and Jerry Greenburg who owned Atco records a subsidiary of Atlantic Records were friends. Mick wanted to make a gospel album. We were asked to participate in the making of the album. We did tell our management that we did not do gospel. We were rhythm and Blues singers. Our managers did not care about that so they sent us to do back-ground singing on one of his songs. The album became a double platinum seller titled "Only Want to Be Your Friend." We never saw a dime from our participation in that album. That album is still playing today. We also did a song with Big Daddy Kane, from which we received a gold album. Never saw any monetary compensation for that work either. Somebody made money from those albums, but it was not us.

Superstar Aretha Franklin did something that I found amusing. During a performance on a PBS television show, she came into the green room with a big pot of collard greens. She immediately announced that the pot was hers and hers alone. She emphatically told everyone in the room that she was not sharing. I thought to myself, damn woman as big as you are you should want to share, with everyone in the room. She was the "Queen of Soul" so she could do what she wanted.

There was another female artist whose name I do not remember except that she had one big record. We were interviewed on the radio station WBLS in New York by Disk Jockey Lenny Green. The station ordered some food for the guest. She was interviewed first by Lenny followed by our group. When we finished our interview, we noticed that this woman who was already physically big had devoured two large pizzas. I saw grease running down her face and on the sides of her mouth along with the remnants of the pizzas. All I could do was laugh through my disgust.

We did a few shows with Earth Wind and Fire and Mandrill where pyrotechnics were used. When on stage we previously did the best that we could to stay clear of the special effects. We knew what was in the ingredients. Finally, we decided to use flash paper that when lit it sparked and disappeared. Since the paper had to be lit, our keyboard player Erskin had a lit cigarette on the edge of his keyboard. Erskin was a hell of a keyboard player who later played with Rick James. We used the cigarette to light the paper. Sometimes we went down into the audience with the flash papers, running down the aisles, wowing the crowd. We had to stop using this action in our show when one time we noticed that Ted's costume was all burnt on the edges of the sleeves. Ted was not performing the action the way we all were taught. He was doing his own thing. His costume was so badly burned that we had to replace it.

We had the privilege to be able to perform on the Arsenio Hall show where I met Sinbad. Both of those brothers were nice guys. I had a picture taken of me with Sinbad and Arsenio only to find out later there was no film in my camera. That was such a disappointment.

I was very comfortable when performing but when it came to being interviewed by people like Dick Clark, I always took the back seat. My brother Vernon would take the lead and shine during these interviews. He was always outgoing and willing to take chances. When we did our shows, it usually was not planned but Vernon took the lead to talk to the audience. He could do it well, I could not. If anyone goes back and watches our television interviews with Don Cornelius on Soul Train you would see how introverted I appeared to be. I saw Don and Dick as bigger than life. They were seen every week on television by millions of admiring people. I was in awe of their power and personalities.

At the Apollo Theatre in New York, we had these flash boxes that would explode at the end of the performance. On one occasion the embers from the blast shot out into the audience and caught fire to the hair of a young man sitting in the front row. He had a big afro hair style which was literally on fire. We watched his hair burn from the stage as he screamed. I thought for sure we were going to get sued. It was the end of the show so we used this action to disappear from the stage like "Magic." We were sitting backstage after the show waiting for the Fire Marshall to arrive when the man whose hair was on fire came backstage. He was so excited to meet us that all he wanted was autographs. We dodged a bullet, no lawsuit. That was the last time we used pyrotechnics. It was time to stop blowing things up. To many things could go wrong, too much liability.

We performed on a television show called "The Midnight Special with Chaka Khan. When we finished the taping of the show we tried to talk to her about watching her money as we tried to do with New Edition. Her management kept her away from us. When she finished her act, she was quickly escorted back to her dressing room. Her singing was unbelievable. Later in life Ted told me that he did have a conversation with her and that out of all the group members she seemed to have been most interested in was me. He gave this information to me sometime later because he knew that if given it sooner, I would have sought her out. I was a womanizer.

Our stage shows were the art of illusion. We knew the audience was fixed on the stage so why not take them on a visual ride, along with the music. Our intention was to include the crowd in what we were doing. Who wanted to come to a show of our type of music where all you saw was a group just standing there and singing? There were many groups with more popular songs than ours. There were groups with gold albums and numerous gold singles, but when they performed on stage all the attention was on the lead singer. This was because the movement of the rest of the group was minimal. Blue Magic did our best to tell a story on stage with our music. It was not called a stage show for nothing. Part of what makes movies interesting is the movement and the emotion. That is what we did. Our shows were an act in which we were the actors. We designed our choreography in such a way that there was so much happening on stage that an individual in the audience could not follow it all. We did so much on stage that most people at the end of a song probably missed something one of us was doing.

There were comical or dirty tricks that our competing contemporaries played on us. The Futures were one of those groups. Blue Magic was always competing against them when we appeared on the same stage. On one occasion after their show, knowing that we were following them on stage they poured water over the stage floor. The band played our intro as we hit the stage. Vernon was the last to come on stage and as he did, he slipped on the wet floor bumping into his microphone which hit him in the face. His reaction to getting smacked by the microphone was to swing back at it. We all just looked at him, laughed and went on with the show.

On another show someone put boogers on my mic. I looked at it and thought to myself that I cannot sing into this microphone. Sometimes we had to put our mouths right on the mic to get the best tone. I quickly found something to wipe the microphone off.

Some of our band members did not feel that they were part of the Blue Magic family. We heard people fighting from our dressing room before one of our performances in Upstate New York. I did not see the fight but I could tell that whoever was fighting was really tearing up the place. I must admit that it was scary. The sounds of the violence seemed to be getting closer to our dressing room. We all agreed that, if necessary, we were going to fight our way out. We were not punks. We were from "North Philly," so we were prepared to do what we had to. Hearing what we were prepared to do, our guitar player, then told us that he did not feel good. A lady working backstage asked him what was wrong? When he told her that he felt sick she called an ambulance. When the ambulance arrived, he was put on a stretcher. As the medics rolled him out of the building, he looked at us and winked. I felt he was saying with his actions "You all stay here and fight, I'm getting out of here!" We did not have to fight, but that was the end of our association with him. He showed no loyalty to our group.

In St. Louis after a performance was over, the promoter paid us and then Invited us to a club. None of us really wanted to go. We all wanted to go back to the hotel and relax. The promoter begged us to come with him, telling us that our fans were expecting to see us. We reluctantly went along. As soon as we got to the club I looked around, and all I saw is what I would describe as thugs. My caution antenna instantly went up. I told the group that we should stay close together as I was carrying our money. I scanned the room and saw guys just looking at us. They were not smiling, and did not appear to be looking at us with admiration. This was another situation where I thought we might have to fight our way out. Thank God we did not have too. When I first met the promoter, I got a vibe that he was not kosher. There was just something about his demeaner that bothered me. I grew up in the street, so I had experience in reading people who were also from the street. While in the club it did cross my mind as to whether we were being set up to be robbed. I wondered whether the promoter was trying to get his money back.

Somewhere out west we shared the stage with Roger Trottman and the Zap Band. During the sound check and rehearsal, I watched what they were doing. I had never seen them before. To say the least they were impressive. They were doing back flips and leaving the stage and changing clothes during the performance. I knew that their stage show was better than ours. What I had experienced in the past with ego driver performers I was not going to let happen to me now. They were magnificent. Once I saw that I went over to Roger and asked him could we go on before his group. I knew that following his on-stage performance was going to be hard to beat. He said no and that he wanted to teach us a lesson. I did not understand that because although we both had hit records, we had never interacted with them before. I never knew what was the cause of the animosity? We were a singing group where Zap was a band that had a new sound using some technology. It was sad that sometime later Roger got into a dispute with his brother who shot and killed him.

Jeffery Osborn the led singer at the time of the band LTD came off stage after their performance, looking frustrated and sad. Noticing this I asked him what was wrong. He told me that he did not like how the band was playing when he sung. He felt that they were playing too loud. He did not feel that he and the band were on the same page musically. I do not know it for a fact but that could have been one of the reasons why he eventually broke away from the band.

During my associations with some famous musicians of color, I noticed their attraction to white women. I do not consider myself to prejudice, the heart wants what the heart wants. I however felt they paraded some of those women around as if they were trophies. Ike Turner was totally disrespectful to Tina. He was so egotistical that he would come down a hallway with two white women on his arms, right in front of her. I saw the same action with a popular singer and bass player, when we were backstage. It was if they were saying this is what you can get when you reach my level of success. I always thought to myself, why two white women, what was that all about? We were exposed to so many beautiful black women of all shapes and sizes. How could they be ignored for women who probably would not look at them twice if they were just average black guys on the street. They seemed to treat these white women as status symbols. We were good friends with one of the original members of a popular singing group. He invited Keith and I to his hotel room on and occasion where he had plenty of cocaine for our consumption. He also had two white women in the room that I felt were there for him to show off. Once again, I thought to myself, what is up with having two white women? Those artists and some others I felt fed into the myth that all black men wanted white woman.

As time marched on, our type of Rhythm and Blues love music began to fade with the introduction of disco music. This music which was high energy dance music started in the late seventies. In my opinion it was a way for white America to be a part of the black experience through dance. That was not the type of music that made us famous. We were Balladeers. The only two up tempo songs that we had were "Look Me Up" and "Welcome to the Club." WMOT now wanted us to sing some songs to keep up with the new trend. They did not consult us at all. Bobby Eli wrote two songs "Mother Funk" and "Freakenstein." They had Vernon record both songs, without consulting the rest of us. They electronically added the background vocals. To show how little control we had over our careers, they put these songs on our next album without our knowledge or permission.

Many of the Rhythm and Blues groups of the sixties and early seventies were killed off because of disco music. The groups with lead male singer who could sing high tenor or falsetto became less popular. With the advent of disco, female singers such as Donna Summers began to replace them. Male tenor singers were no longer popular or needed. Groups such as the O Jay's, the Temptations and the Whispers continued to be popular because they had baritone singers. Our status as a group dropped, because of this new age music. I understood what was happening because our music replaced that of groups like the Drifters and the Platters who came before us. Motown was even beginning to fade in popularity at this time.

CHAPTER 12
" WELCOME BACK "

Living back in Philadelphia after separating from Doctor York, I constantly visited my mother's home where Vernon and I talked. I asked him had he heard from any of the guys in the group. When he told me that they broke up I started to imagine the possibility of us getting back together. I found out Rick was living with his mother; Ted was working in a Ladies clothing store and Keith was living in New Jersey. I did not understand why a singing group who had a gold album and who were all living reasonably close to each other would not be performing.

I went to see Ted first at the store where he was working. We talked for a while and I presented him with my proposal. He said yes to our getting the group back together. Rick was next since he lived right around the corner from my mother. He said OK. Vernon and I talked to Keith who also wanted our reunion, so in 1978 we became Blue Magic again.

Shortly after the group all agreed to get back together, I called our old band leader Tony Bethel. I asked him if he could get the old band back together. His answered me "Not a Problem." Tony played the trumpet. I then started booking the shows myself, using various booking agencies. One agency that I used on many occasions was named Lady of Troy. She was able to book us in shows all over the country. In my mind, I thanked Doctor York for all the organizational knowledge that he gave me in the year that I spent with him.

I took what I learned and made it work for Blue Magic the second time around. I tried to clear up any feelings that I had as it related to the breakup of our group. It was time for us to be mature and move on. It was time for us to make some money doing what we did best. I called everyone up for rehearsals when we had a job. There was never any problem with my taking the lead. Everyone wanted to make money.

Rick at some point started missing rehearsals and shows. He eventually just walked away. He told us that he did not want to perform any more. He never said it to me but either Ted or Vernon was told that he wanted to start a family and do something else with his life. No one wanted him to go but that was his decision, so we moved on without him. I will admit that many of the clubs that had formally booked us stopped, simply because it was now the disco era. It was rough financially sometimes, but I wanted us to continue.

There was a producer, who knew Ted. He was one of Russell Simmon's producers. When we met him, he told us that Russell was a fan of our music. He also told us that Russell wanted to meet with us to possibly collaborate on an album. No one had to think twice so we said yes. We agreed to the album and started driving up to the Bronx from Philadelphia where the studio was located. I heard that Russell put up one hundred and thirty thousand dollars to make the album. We got along well with the producer and his engineer while making the album. The producer knew these two rappers who owned an Exotic car. We used that car on the album cover. The producer bought all our clothes for the cover. We were dressed in these nice yellow suits. On the front of the album cover we were seen standing around this beautiful car. On the back of the cover, you see us in the same positions without the car. I always thought it was a nice album cover.

This producer was from the street so he knew people who knew people. Someone told him that Ted was trying to sell his yellow suit, from the album cover, on the streets of Brooklyn. That was his first Inkling that Ted may have had financial problems.

We completed the album and we were happy with the result. Since we had previous experience as to how the music business operated, we noticed that our record was not being played. Not even the disk jockeys in New Jersey on the local stations were playing our record. Stores did not have the album for sale. When an album is promoted, it goes out to radio stations and everywhere that records were sold. Our album was only given out to a chosen few. We also did a video related to the album. The song we performed on the video was called "It's Like Magic." Pam Grier and Max Julian were hired to act out a scene on the film. We taped our whole performance of the song in advance. When the video was cut and edited what you saw most of was the two stars. It was our album being promoted but we were just background players. We did another music video to another song from the album called "Romeo and Juliet." I thought it was a silly song. We filmed the video in a park in Brooklyn. There were a lot of children playing in the park at the time. They danced in the video. Once again, we were the background noise. We did not complain much about how the video was produced and directed. We had never done videos before so I found it exciting. I think we were using so many drugs at the time that we did not give a damn. We spoke to Russell about our concerns and we got no real answers as to why the album was not being promoted more aggressively. I spoke to someone experienced in the business end of music, and he suggested that the album might have been used as a tax write off. I never had any proof that is what happened but it did make sense. During most of our association with him, Russell could not have been a nicer person. I remember him traveling with us on a bus to do a show.

We were now performing regularly again. To do something different we added dancers to the show. Never did that before. I decided to start a Blue Magic fan club. I sold memberships at our shows for a few dollars.

Russell set up a show for us at Sweetwaters, a popular club in Manhattan. He invited top people in the music business to enjoy the show. He reserved tables for them right up front. Ted was a no show for the performance. We had no idea what happened to him or what to do since he was our lead singer. Singer Allison Williams, who was among Russell's guests was there. She was also signed to his label. We had to come out on stage and announce that our lead singer was not with us. I looked down at Russell and saw a look on his face that said "Are You Serious!" Allison was gracious enough to come up on stage, and sing some of our hit songs such as "What's Come Over Me." The other songs we got audience participation. Ted never explained to us why he did not show up. We were all doing drugs but that did not stop us from showing up to do a show. Russell dropped us after that show. I did not blame him for that decision. He just told us "You all got to go!" That was the end of that relationship. I understood how he felt. We were not dependable.

A few years after collaboration ended with Russell, I heard that he was making an appearance at Macys in New York City. He was walking with his entourage and from a roped off area I yelled to him, "Hey Russell What's Happening?" He spoke but I do not think that he recognized me. I was hurt. I did get a chance to meet with him for several minutes later where he did remember me. I was offended that he did not originally recognize me. My girlfriend who was with me, was very supportive during that encounter. She saw the expression of hurt and disappointment on my face. I believe that the reason Russell was not warm towards me, still had to do with the past embarrassing positions my group placed him in, none of which was my fault.

An interesting story took place when the whole group was using drugs during our second time around. Vernon had gotten married and was now living in New York. He was asked to go to the Universal Booking company and pick up the money that we were owed. He told me that he could pick up the money but he was not coming down to Philadelphia until the next week. I told him that Ted was in New York so he should give the money to him because I knew he was coming back to Philadelphia sooner. Vernon being aware of Ted's drug use questioned me "Are you sure that you want me to give Ted your money?" The Christmas holidays were rapidly approaching so we all needed our money. The money was given to Ted. Two days go by after Ted was given the money and we had not heard from him. A week goes by and still no word from Ted. Keith and I were talking constantly about the situation. Ted was living with him at that time and he had not heard from him either. Another week passed and Ted showed up at my home. "Here is your money, "he said as he handed it to me. He then told me that he did not have Keith's money because he spent it on crack. I knew that this was a problem that Keith was not going to overlook. He had already told me that if Ted did not have his money, he was going to kill him. I thought that he was serious. I knew that Keith's brother Big Don, who was the leader of the Morocco gang, would have urged and assisted him in that felony. I decided to tell him to give my money to Keith. I knew what was going to happen. I decided to sacrifice my children's Christmas to save his life and keep Keith from going to jail. My kids did not get much for Christmas that year because I wanted to preserve the group. I heard that Ted caught hell when he got to the home he and Keith shared. I could only imagine what would have happened to him without the money. He did deserve whatever happened to him.

Our lead singer's pattern of behavior, missing or coming late to shows continued. It was obvious to me that Illegal drugs had taken over his life. We did not want him to leave the group, even with his irresponsible behavior. He was our lead singer. He made that decision on his own. I do not have proof but I believe that people were in his head telling him that he was the group. They may have even pointed out to him that he sung all the hit records and that he did not need the other group members. It did not help that he was using drugs regularly. He just told us one day that he was leaving. Ted's last show with us was in New Jersey in 1989.

We had just performed a show at Sweetwater. While there we heard a guy sing who sounded just like Ted. His name was Rod Wayne. Once Ted left it took us about a month to locate Ron. Vernon's wife Elaine, was helpful in finding him and convincing him to join our group. He told us that he would love to be a part of Blue Magic. There was an Instant musical connection with our new lead singer so we did not miss a beat when performing without Ted.

We were preparing to performed a show in Manhattan within a year of Ted's leaving. During our sound check Ted showed up and told us that he wanted to sing with our group again. He even tried singing over Rod during the rehearsal. I had to tell him to stop. I was still hurt over the way he abandoned the group. I told him no. He left the rehearsal with his head down. We were torn as a group over the decision we made since he had been our original lead singer. During the past year he tried to bill himself as Ted Mills the original lead singer of Blue Magic. He was not very successful. Ted was never good at handling business. When he was with our group, we never allowed him to handle our business. That was not his forte.

Among the many responsibilities I took on after reforming our group was booking the shows and collecting our pay checks. I was using a lot of drugs at the time, and as a result I started messing up the money. Crack was calling me again, so I made the decision to ask Vernon to take over my responsibilities. I told him that I would give him all my booking contacts. All I asked for was a five percent commission off each booking. Vernon agreed. He did one or two shows before he came to me and told me that he was turning this work over to someone else. He justified his decision by telling me that he thought someone could handle our management better because they had a better business sense. All due respect to Vernon, I never thought my brother was a good leader. On the other hand, I thought that the person he chose was a leader. This person took over the business management. That was a lasting mistake. Eventually my five percent went away. The next thing that was done was there were now added on little expenses that took money away from the rest of the group. We were being charged for small things like paper clips and faxes. It got to the point that I was so angry that I did not want to go into a room with our new business manager and Vernon because I thought we would end up physically fighting. It was hard for me to phantom that my brother would go along with allowing this to happening me. It got so bad that our business manager was charging the group for personal cell phone bills. When we questioned these expenses, we were given some bogus excuse for paying the bills. I was starting to get fed up with this behavior which was not in my best financial interest. The manager even wanted a booking fee even when they did not book the show. If the booking fee might have gone to someone else such as Universal booking, they then wanted a management fee. The manager was smart but was also controlling.

There came a time when Keith and I could no longer take how we were being treated. Universal Booking had a practice of not giving artists a deposit until after they performed. I understood why they adopted that practice because there were artists who would not show up. The business manager tried using this practice on us when on one occasion Keith asked for an advance on money deposited in our account. He was told that the money in the account was not his money until after we performed.

We were looking for another lead singer. Vernon found a singer that was good. He was the whole package as a showman. Sadly, off stage we found him to be strange. He did not smile, and sometimes during conversations his mind seemed to be somewhere else. On stage he could do it all but off stage he was in a different world from the rest of us.

Keith and I decided that it was time to assert our power within the group. A female from our fan club gave someone she knew a reference to join group. He sent us a video tape of his singing. His name was Moe. We were impressed with his singing. The only problem was that Moe looked like the white image of Jesus Christ. He was tall light skin with dreadlock hair and a long grey beard. Moe came from the church where I guess his appearance did not matter. I told him that he had to change the way he looked. He cut his hair and shaved his beard. Moe's real name is Fernando Kee. He told us that his last name was shorten from Cherokee because of his American Indian heritage.

Once we started rehearsing, I noticed that although he could sing, he did not have any stage persona. He was kind of stiff. I must admit that Vernon's singer had a much better stage presence. We were scheduled to do show at a place called Tomasina's in Queens New York. We argued over who should take the lead during that show. Vernon eventually agreed to let my guy sing. It did not go well. Moe just did not have that showmanship that would wow the crowd, especially the ladies. Vernon won that round. Moe did continue to sing with our group. He still sings with my group today. He has developed a much better stage presence over the years and he definitely can sing.

Things continued to be tense between Vernon on one side and Keith and I on the other. The climax of my working with my brother came in Washington DC in 2005. Our road manager who had been with us a long time came to pick Keith and I up for the show. In our attempt at a power play, both of us told him that we were not performing. Moe got to the concert hall early on his own.

Vernon was already there and told Moe that he was out as a member of the group. He was pissed, so they started arguing. We were supposed to perform along with the Chi Lites. When Keith and I did not hear back from Bobby we thought that it best that we drive down to Washington. I heard Moe and Vernon arguing as I approached the dressing room. What I did not know was that Vernon had called a former member of the Delphonics singing group in advance and a guy who sung with us in the past to replace Keith and I. He taught these singers our choreography in anticipation of our rebellion. I think he had already made up his mind that he no longer wanted to work with us. To my shock and disappointment, he told Keith, Moe, and myself that we were not going on stage. That move showed how much power Keith thought he had at that time. Keith was so mad that he wanted to tear up the dressing room full of our clothes. I stopped him from doing it, although I understood his anger. I did not know it at the time but the split was going to be good for us. We drove back to New York without any further incidents.

We now had to start from scratch putting a group back together. We still had the right to call ourselves Blue Magic. That meant finding singers, replacing our clothes, and putting a new band together. Our first move was to find people who wanted to sing with us. The first singer we recruited was Wade Elliot. He had sung with us before, so we were familiar with his style. He had everything that we wanted in a singer, good looks, and stage presence. The women went crazy over him. We then added Moe back into the mix. The group now consisted of Keith Wade, Moe, and myself. Since we lost all our wardrobes, we decided that we would all wear black suits and black shoes. I then taught Carol how to manage the group. I gave her all my contacts and walked her through booking the shows, talking with the promoters, and getting the contracts. She was a natural. She was a quick study. Once we started getting some deposits towards shows we bought clothes off the rack to wear on stage.

One of our group members started having problems with alcohol. He was just drinking too much. During performances he would go out on stage lay on the floor and take his shoes off while singing. The first time we ever got booed was at a show in Washington DC. When I picked him up for that show from his house, he was already drunk and fighting with his girlfriend. I knew then that we were in trouble. He was the man as a entertainer. The adulation from the fans however went to his head. He even told us one time that the people came to see him not the group. I answered him by saying that he should put his name on the marquee alone and see how many people come to the show. When he made that acknowledgment, I knew it was time for him to go. We did a couple more shows with him. On our way to West Virginia, to do one of those shows he was drinking in the car. When we stopped for gas, I took his liquor bottle and hid it. I did not know how he did it but he found the bottle. On another occasion I was pulled aside at a show by a member of the group Heat Wave. He told me that a member of my group was drunk. This only shows how serious the problem had become. He was right because when he went out on stage, he was slurring his speech and forgot the words to some of our songs. The next day we received a terrible write-up in a Washington newspaper. The articles accused him of using drugs.

The next person we auditioned was Ivory Bell. I personally never liked him. I do not remember why I did not like him. I just think it was a vibe that I felt at the time. He did not last long with our group

Then there was the audition of a lead singer, who was a chronic liar. The first lie he told was on me which did not endear me to him. I told him that our rehearsal was at 3'o Clock. He was late arriving. While standing outside our rehearsal hall smoking a cigarette at four in the afternoon, he told Keith that I told him that the rehearsal started at four thirty. He did several shows with us although he did not have Ted's sound. A member of the singing group The Intruders, Big Mack warned me about him being a liar, but we had to find out for ourselves.

Then we auditioned a fellow that had been one of Ted's background singers. Ted had let him go. When performing with us on one occasion he spent time on stage watching me rather than singing. Keith had to tell him to sing. We were going to California so I explained to him that he had to sound like Ted Mills. He had a nice voice, but he was strange. He answered my request by telling me that he could not do it. He started crying on the phone. I knew then why Ted let him go. He was just too soft. Maybe he just had stage fright.

We performed with everyone during our resurgence. The Stylistics, the Dramatics. Black Ivory and the Delfonics among others. We never did the black college circuit. We did perform one time at Howard University in Washington DC.

While performing on a cruise we met the mother of Sean "Puffy" Combs. I found her to be an attractive woman. We socialized with her a great deal while on the ship. All the time with her I was thinking about a way to get an introduction to her famous son." I do not do that; it is my son's business and I do not get involved," she graciously told me. Nothing beats failure except not trying, I tried.

When crossing the border into Canada to perform, Keith and one of our band members were taken into custody by the border police. Keith was arrested because he either lost his passport or it was stolen, and the person in possession of his identification was wanted for a few murders. The only thing that saved Keith was that the person committing the crimes was described as missing two fingers on one hand. Keith had all his fingers. The band member was arrested because there was a warrant for him accusing him of bestiality. We left him with the police and moved on to perform. I never knew what happened to him. He never worked with us again.

CHAPTER 13
"LOOK ME UP"

There were things that happened to me in my life that were unrelated to my association with Blue Magic. Some can be explained and some cannot.

While living in Jamaica, New York there was a time when I started feeling weak. I could not explain it but my condition got progressively worse. My girlfriend took me to Queens General Hospital near our apartment, where I was diagnosed with having a bleeding ulcer. The doctors told me that blood was running down to my feet and not through my body. The next thing that happened was that I was transported to a room where a doctor explained to me that he had to put a tube down my throat attached to camera so that he could locate the exact place of the ulcer. My immediate reaction was to say "WHAT!?" He told me to open my mouth and just swallow. Although it only took a few minutes it seemed like hours. Once inside my mouth he said, "OK I see it." That was the most uncomfortable medical procedures that I ever experienced. He then told me that to cure me surgery was required. They then put me to sleep. When I awoke, I was in room alone with an intravenous tube sticking out of my arm and a heart monitor beeping. A priest walked into the room and asked me "Are you alright my son?" I thought that he thought that I was close to death. I did find out that if I had not gotten treatment for that problem, I would have died, which explained the urgency for surgery.

I had a terrible headache for about a week on another occasion. My girlfriend took me to Queens Hospital again, where the emergency room doctor told me that he thought that I had bacterial meningitis. He then decided that he had do a spinal tap which required a long needle being inserted in my spine. He explained to me that fluid would then be drawn. He prepared me and stuck the needle in my spine. No sedative and nothing to numb me. The doctor told me to hold still and warned me that if I moved, I could end up paralyzed. It was a painful experience. I screamed so loud that I am sure it was heard throughout the hospital. I heard the doctor say "Hold on I think I got it!" I then saw this yellow fluid that was drawn from my spine. While I was in the hospital a very nice nurse came into my room and asked me," Baby who stressed you out?" I immediately thought back to recently watching my live- in girlfriend get out of a black car that was driven by an unknown man. My first thought was that she was cheating on me. I did not think that what I saw was that stressful but maybe it was. I thought to myself how could I have contracted a disease from stress? Later in life I understood how stress could affect the body's immune system.

I always had problems with my stomach. I suffered from acid reflux. Around the age of twenty-three I went to a doctor to get help with this problem when I could no longer tolerate the pain. I could not believe that he told me that my problem was that in Africa there were no cows, so my African ancestors never drank cow's milk. He basically told me that my illness was hereditary based on my ancestry even though I was not a big milk drinker. He consequently gave me no medication for my condition. I believed him at the time, I did not know any better. I continued to suffer at times. Later in life when I thought about it, I could not believe that a trained medical doctor, who was black would diagnose my problem that way. I was young and did not understand that maybe I should have gotten a second opinion.

When I was young boy, and even today I have been able to peel skin away from parts of my body. My mother took me to a doctor who told us that I was allergic to penicillin. The problem with that diagnosis is that I had never taken the drug. I do not think that he knew the cause of my problem so he just made something up. I always thought that those prognosis are the results of incompetent physicians. I did not have great medical insurance so you get what you pay for.

I have learned many things about life over the past six decades. First and most important I have a better understanding of self. The more one understands about self the more comfortable you become with yourself. I have thought long and hard about my life. I have accepted the good and the bad making it easy for me to realize my self- worth. I understand that because I have been fortunate enough to have associated with many famous and influential people, it does makes me unique. I can only hope that by reading my story it will enlighten and maybe help someone avoid the pitfall that I experienced.

One of the areas that I have strong feeling about are the relationships between men and women. Men think differently than woman. It took more than half of my life to figure that out. It is my opinion that young men put too high a priority on the physical aspects of a potential partner. I was no exception as a young man. I never thought much about compatibility in my women, only what attracted me to them physically. While on the road all those years the only thing I really wanted from women that I met was sex. I had a wife at home or was always in a long-term relationship, but that was not enough. Admittedly not understanding myself, that was shallow thinking. I had to learn that being friends with a woman is the strongest bond that I can have. Friends first, sex second. I believe that men and women in too many cases have a different interpretation of love.

I have a cynical opinion of America. Racism has always been here and unfortunately it is still alive and well. Economically disadvantaged people are still valued less in this society. Black people no matter what they have achieved I believe are still called nigger in some circles. I am sure that President Obama was called nigger by some.

This is violent country. There are too many guns and people too willing to use them. Unfortunately, too many of our young black men use violence as a method of deciding dispute. They use a gun at as a means of power. Unfortunately that firearm may be the only power that they feel that they possess. What they do not understand is that attitude and behavior plays right into the hands of those who want to control and destroy us as a race of people. There should not be any secret in America as to why firearms are so readily available. Too many young black people do not know the history of this country and our relationship to slavery and the Jim crow south. I believe that to many young black men especially in lower economically deprived neighborhood, have very little hope of being a success in this society. This society has done very little to show them anything different. A perfect example of this is the relationship between the police and the black community. All these years later we are still discussing this problem.

I spend my free time now when not performing reading. I enjoy books about psychology. They have helped me better understand the relationship between how I was raised and the things that I have experienced.

To my regret I am not in touch with any of my children accept my youngest daughter. My contact with my youngest brother and my sister has been minimal.

The current members of Blue Magic are Fernando Key we call him "Big Moe" Buddy Williams who we call "Buddy Love," and Elzie Ross. We are still performing and enjoying the occasional road trips.

My close friend and original member of Blue Magic Keith Beaton passed away on January 13 2023. He suffered for a long time from liver damage, which I attributed to all the years of heavy alcohol drinking. He performed with our group long as he could before his health failed. I looked at recent pictures taken of our group where everyone looked happy but him. Knowing him the way that I have for decades I could see in his eyes how he knew that his health was failing. I was sorry to see him go but at the same time glad he is gone because he was suffering. We had so many good times together. He was truly my brother.

Original member of Blue magic Richard Pratt passed away in the spring of 2021. He also was a good brother and a good friend. We created some beautiful music together. I will miss him always.

There are only three original members of our group still alive, lead singer Ted Mills, my brother Vernon Sawyer, and myself.

The recent Covid 19 Pandemic slowed our performing. It has been rough on me personally and financially. This past couple of years has been the longest time in recent history when I did not perform regularly. When not performing I miss the road and the crowd. It is what I do.

Since I have had a great deal of free time on my hands, I began to examine my life. When we started working on this book my life was going well. Then came the pandemic putting a strain on my money, followed by my woman of fifteen years wanting me to move out. I consequently found that writing this book helped me to cope with the negative situations that I was experiencing. It was the right time. My spiritual side told me that this book was an answer to a prayer. I believe that God would not have taken away the one thing that I did best unless he was replacing it with something good. God has taken me this far and he continues to not let me down. I thank God for looking out for me during my successes and failures. It is my hope that by telling my story in the form of a book it will lead me to better days ahead. At the start of my luck going bad I wrote down on a piece of paper something that I looked at everyday "Control your emotions, your mind, and your thoughts!" I would not allow myself to think negatively. I realize that negative thoughts lead to negative feeling about myself. Such emotions can put you on the road to destruction. I refuse to allow that to happen to me. I remembered how my lack of self- control led me to do many stupid things as a young man. I refuse to repeat me past. I believe that the spirit is testing me, and I refuse to fail the test. My belief in myself and my willingness to survive will pull me through as it has always done.

Probably one of my biggest regrets is the money that I lost as result of my poor business sense, and drug use. As a young man I was a perfect example of what can happened to someone who had very little or no guidance when it comes to money matters. I have seen this happened to many people in the sports and music industries. I know that I lost millions because of poor money management.

I have tried to be a better person as I have aged. When I was young and had a pocket full of money, I never thought much about that. I would like to leave this life with a positive legacy.

—

BLUE MAGIC SONGS

ALL I REALLY NEED IS YOU

ANSWER TO MY PRAYER

CHASING RAINBOWS

FEELIN THE LOVE

GRATEFUL

LAND OF MAKE BELIEVE

LET THERE BE LOVE

LOOK ME UP

LOVE HAS FOUND IT'S WAY TO ME

IT'S LIKE MAGIC

SIDESHOW

SPELL

STILL IN LOVE WITH YOU

SIT ALONE AGAIN

TALKING TO MYSELF

TEAR IT DOWN

THREE RING CIRCUS

THE LONELIEST HOUSE ON THE BLOCK

WHEN YA COMING HOME

WHAT'S COME OVER ME

BLUE MAGIC ALBUMS

BLUE MAGIC　　　1974

THIRTEEN BLUE MAGIC LANE　1975

FROM OUT OF THE BLUE　1974

WELCOME BACK　2010

LIVE IN PHILLY　2010

MYSTIC DRAGON　2013

MESSAGE FROM MAGIC　2019

SIDESHOW LYRICS

Come in take a chair

Nothing to do out there

Is what you want what you need

Decisions made in Privacy

Step right up and name your game

Take a chance pick a card - any card

I'll guess your age – I'll name you fate

Dedication

To original members of Blue Magic and lifelong friends Keith Beaton and Richard Pratt.

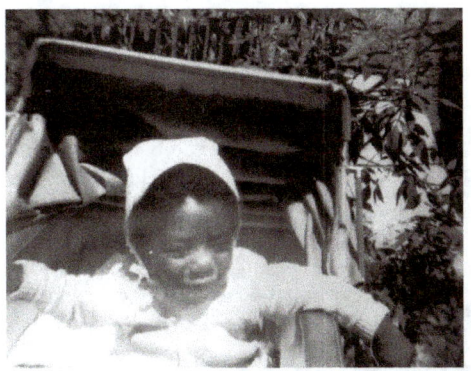

Baby Wendell

Me smiling in my grade school picture
while attending Bach Elementary in
Philadelphia, PA.

My dad,
Weldon Sawyer
and my mom,
Mattie Sawyer,
dressed to the nines.
They were our
biggest supporters.

The day I married Brenda Sawyer (Brown) and
my family celebrating this special occasion
with me. From left, Vernon Sawyer (brother),
Lorraine Perry (my sister), Mattie Sawyer
(mom), Weldon Sawyer (dad), myself and
Michael Sawyer (brother).

The original members
of Blue Magic before
a show in 1973. (From
left) Keith Beaton,
Richard Pratt, Ted
Mills, Vernon Sawyer
and myself.

Ike and Tina Dismiss Local Group, Blue Magic, During European Tour

Area Singers Say Ike, Tina Were 'Jealous'

By PAUL A. BENNETT
(O) The Trenton State

For no apparent reason other than jealousy, Ike Turner, the other half of the "Ike and Tina Turner Review," fired a young group of Philadelphia singers and barred them from completing a scheduled 16-concert European tour the group was doing with the Review. His only obvious reason: "We were too good," the group claims.

Blue Magic, five young men (ranging in age from 21-26) all from North Philadelphia, whose hit record "Spell" brought them much attention, were getting second billing on the tour and from the first concert on, captivated the hearts of the Europeans to the point where the audience wanted to hear them instead of the headlining Review.

According to Blue Magic manager, Al Rubino, who was on the tour, the show would get off to a good start with Blue Magic as the "warm-up" group. When Ike Turner and his band would play, the show dragged and the audience "whistled" (which is the European equivalent of an American "boo").

Then the show would pick up again when Ike's wife and partner Tina, would do her number. Halfway through the tour (after the eighth concert in Cologne, Germany), Ike's ego compelled him to dismiss the group and the message came down to Blue Magic's management to pack
(Continued on Page 6, Col. 1)

HAILING FROM North Philadelphia, these five young men known as "Blue Magic" captivated the hearts of many young lovers with their smash record, "Spell". With other big hits such as "Guess Who", Blue Magic won the hearts of audiences all over Europe and un-intentionally stole the show from the headlining Ike and Tina Turner Review. For their hard work and efforts, Ike Turner reportedly fired them off the tour and sent them dejectedly back home. Seated is Vernon Sawyer. From L. to r.: Wendell Sawyer, Keith Beaton, Richard Pratt, and Ted Mills.

Newspaper article
describing Blue Magic's
experience during
the Ike & Tina Tour
in Berlin, Germany.
Suspicion grew when
our time on stage
was cut as local fans
cheered for us. Let's
just say we overstayed
our welcome.

The original members of Blue Magic posing for a photo with Luther Vandross and fans.

Blue Magic's first album. From that moment on, we became a household name performing coast to coast.

The soulful vocal group, The Futures. One of the most popular Philly groups we battled to top the charts.

One of Motown's innovative vocal groups, Dynamic Superiors. Straight out of Washington D.C, they were tough competition.

The current members of Blue Magic before we hit the stage at our show in Winter of 2023. From left, Elie Ross, Robert Williams (lead singer), myself and Fernando Kee.

Dr. Cornell West and I at an event in his honor. It felt great to know such an iconic figure was a big fan of Blue Magic.

Chris Rock and I at a show in Philadelphia, PA.

I was honored to have my
shine on the red carpet at
the National R&B Music
Society event. Blue Magic
is still being recognized
after 50 years.

The original
members of Blue
Magic reunited
a few years ago.
Our story aired on
TV One's Unsung
Season 12 in 2018.

Anthony Johnson and
I having some fun at his
family's barbeque
in Philadelphia, PA.